FLOWER REMEDIES

CHRISTINE WILDWOOD is an internationally renowned Bach Flower practitioner, aromatherapist and author. She has written many books on herbal medicine, aromatherapy and stress reduction, and she lectures in the USA, Australia, Canada and throughout Europe.

THE SERIES

New Perspectives provide attractive and accessible introductions to a comprehensive range of mind, body and spirit topics. Beautifully designed and illustrated, these practical books are written by experts in each subject.

Titles in the series include:

ALEXANDER TECHNIQUE
by Richard Brennan

MASSAGE
by Stewart Mitchell

AROMATHERAPY
by Christine Wildwood

MEDITATION
by David Fontana

DREAMS
by David Fontana

NLP
by Carol Harris

FENG SHUI
by Man-Ho Kwok with Joanne O'Brien

NUMEROLOGY
by Rodford Barrat

FLOWER REMEDIES
by Christine Wildwood

REFLEXOLOGY
by Inge Dougans

HOMEOPATHY
by Peter Adams

TAROT
by A T Mann

New Perspectives

FLOWER REMEDIES

An Introductory Guide to Natural Healing with Flower Essences

CHRISTINE WILDWOOD

ELEMENT

Shaftesbury, Dorset • Boston, Massachusetts
Melbourne, Victoria

Designed for Element Books Limited by
Design Revolution, Queens Park Villa,
30 West Drive, Brighton, East Sussex BN2 2GE

ELEMENT BOOKS LIMITED
Editorial Director: Sarah Sutton
Editorial Manager: Jane Pizzey
Commissioning Editor: Grace Cheetham
Production Director: Roger Lane

DESIGN REVOLUTION
Editorial Director: Ian Whitelaw
Art Director: Lindsey Johns
Editor: Julie Whitaker
Designer: Vanessa Good

Printed and bound in Great Britain by
Bemrose Security Printing, Derby

British Library Cataloguing in Publication
data available

Library of Congress Cataloging in Publication
data available

ISBN 1-86204-664-6

CONTENTS

ACKNOWLEDGEMENTS

With many thanks to all at Mount Vernon and to everyone else who contributed in some way to the birth of this book. And to Dr Edward Bach whose shining spirit lives on through his work.

NOTE FROM THE PUBLISHER
Any information given in any book in the New Perspectives series is not intended to be taken as a replacement for medical advice. Any person with a condition requiring medical attention should consult a qualified medical practitioner or suitable therapist.

WHAT ARE THE BACH
FLOWER REMEDIES?

CHAPTER ONE

The 38 Flower Remedies that comprise the Bach Flower pharmacopoeia are made from wild flowers that have been carefully selected for their special ability to promote self-healing. For nearly 60 years, wild flowers have been selected and prepared at the Bach Centre at Mount Vernon, Oxfordshire, England, to make these beautiful healing remedies. It was here that the visionary physician Edward Bach lived and worked.

ABOVE FRESHLY PICKED WILD FLOWERS ARE USED TO MAKE THE BACH REMEDIES. PLANTS GROWING IN THE WILD HAVE BEEN NURTURED BY THE LIVING EARTH.

Dr Edward Bach (1886–1936) studied medicine and worked as a bacteriologist and homeopath. He became convinced, however, that poisonous substances of animal, plant or mineral origin should play no part in healing – not even when used in infinitesimal doses as in homeopathy. Much to the chagrin of the British medical establishment, he was inspired (for there is no other word for it) to give up his lucrative London practice and move to North Wales to seek a completely new form of healing – one that was totally benign to both humans and animals.

Bach's homeopathic background had made him aware that highly diluted medicinal substances, so diluted that the original material cannot be detected in the laboratory, can trigger a powerful healing effect in the body. This knowledge was to influence the development of his own system of healing. Equally important to Bach was the realization that long-term stress resulting from emotions such as anger, fear or worry lowered a person's resistance to disease, making the body prey to all manner of infection or illness. Moreover, he believed that an individual's emotional outlook influenced the course, severity and duration of their disease. He also noticed that people suffering from the same disease and sharing similar personalities responded well to a particular remedy, but that others of a varying temperament needed different treatment, although they were suffering from the same physical complaint. Thus Bach's axiom became, 'Take no notice of the disease, think only of the personality of the one in distress'.

Bach was essentially guided by intuition, or what some might call divine inspiration. He believed strongly that the key to the art of true healing lay not in the laboratory but within the plant kingdom, and that these special plants could be found growing wild, nurtured by the living Earth and energized by the synergy of fresh air, water and sunlight.

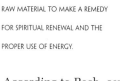

ABOVE THE OLIVE TREE PROVIDES THE RAW MATERIAL TO MAKE A REMEDY FOR SPIRITUAL RENEWAL AND THE PROPER USE OF ENERGY.

8

According to Bach, certain flowers are of a 'higher order' and hold a greater power than those ordinary medicinal plants that heal the body from a biochemical level. The true healing plants, he believed, address disharmony within the mental and spiritual aspects of our being. They transmute negative emotions such as fear, melancholy, and hatred into courage, joy, and love; and in this manner, they correct the cause of our ills.

A Simple Method of Potentization

Bach believed that the early morning dew that rested upon a flower must contain some of its vital properties. He tested his theory by collecting the dew from certain flowers and trying it out on himself. Through his finely developed senses, he found that the dew held a definite power of some kind. Moreover, dew collected from flowers exposed to sunlight was far more potent than that collected from flowers growing in the shade. Bach also found that the essential energies of a plant were concentrated in the flower at full maturity, that is, when it has reached its peak of perfection and is about to fall.

Since collecting large amounts of dew was obviously impractical, Bach devised two methods to enable him to extract the healing properties of plants in the quantities required. These two methods of extraction – or 'potentization' as Bach preferred to call it – are known as the Sun Method and the Boiling Method.

In the Sun Method, the best flower heads are carefully picked. These are then put in a thin, clear glass or crystal bowl filled with spring water. The bowl is then placed on the ground (near the parent plants) where it is exposed to strong sunlight for a few hours. The flowers are then carefully removed with a twig or leaf, thus avoiding human contact with the vitalized water or 'essence'. The essence is then poured into bottles that are half-filled with brandy (which acts as a preservative). This is known as the 'Mother Tincture'.

RIGHT THE SUN METHOD OF GENTLE POTENTIZATION INVOLVES PLACING FLOWER HEADS IN SPRING WATER AND ALLOWING THE SUN TO DO ITS WORK.

LEFT THE BOILING METHOD OF EXTRACTION, IN WHICH THE MATERIAL IS SIMMERED IN SPRING WATER, WAS DEVELOPED BY BACH FOR CERTAIN TYPES OF PLANT.

For blooms, such as Star of Bethlehem, Willow and Elm, that required a stronger method of extraction, Bach devised the Boiling Method. With this method, plant material, such as buds, cones or flowers, is placed in an enamel pan of spring water and simmered for half-an-hour. Afterwards, the pan is covered and left to cool. Then, when cold, the essence is filtered and, as in the previous method, preserved in equal quantities of brandy and labelled 'Mother Tincture'.

The next stage in the preparation, whether using the Sun or the Boiling Method, is to dilute the Mother Tincture in a further quantity of brandy. This bottle is labelled 'Stock Concentrate', and it is in this form that the Remedies are usually sold.

Two of the 38 Flower Remedies are a little different because they are not prepared from European wild flowers. These are Rock Water (potentized spring water) and Cerato, which is a cultivated plant native to the Himalayas.

LEFT CHILDREN RESPOND WELL TO FLOWER REMEDIES. SINCE THE REMEDIES ARE NON-TOXIC, THEY HAVE NO SIDE-EFFECTS AND CAN SAFELY BE USED.

FLOWER REMEDIES IN PRACTICE

The Remedies are prepared from non-poisonous flowers and unpolluted water, and so unlike drugs or herbal remedies proper, an overdose would be totally harmless. They are non-addictive and can be taken by adults, children, and infants alike. Furthermore, many Bach users have found the Remedies beneficial to animals – and even plants – which, of course, dispels the placebo myth so often espoused by sceptics.

To use Flower Remedies successfully, we need to move away from the habit of thinking in terms of physical symptoms. Simply because a Flower Remedy has helped a friend's eczema as well as her anxiety, it does not follow that the same prescription will help your skin problem. It is important to choose the correct Remedy, or combination of Remedies, to match your specific emotional needs. As we

ABOVE HOLLY IS USED FOR THOSE WHO ARE JEALOUS, SUSPICIOUS OR FULL OF HATRED FOR OTHERS.

have seen, Bach recognized 38 healing flowers, one for each of the most common negative states of mind that darken our perception. Each Remedy transmutes the negative outlook into its opposite or positive aspect. Holly, for example, is the Remedy for those who harbour hatred, envy, or suspicion. A course of this Remedy will enable such a person to give without wanting anything in return, and to rejoice in the good fortune of others.

More often than not, however, few people are as true to type as these examples suggest. Most require a mixture of Flower Remedies to deal with the various negative aspects that may be predominant, especially in cases of deep-rooted physical and emotional disharmony (*see* chapter 3, pp.21–32).

11

COMPLEMENTARY AND PREVENTATIVE

Although Bach was an idealist, he was not unrealistic. He would have been the first to employ other forms of treatment when necessary to support the action of the Flower Remedies. However, the Bach Flower Remedies are a wonderful adjunct to all other forms of treatment, be it allopathy (orthodox medicine), homeopathy, herbalism, acupuncture, aromatherapy and such like. They work on the mental/spiritual level and will not interfere with any other means of healing the body – in fact, they enhance other forms of treatment.

The Bach Remedies reign supreme in the area of preventative treatment. Indeed, it is far better to use them in this manner than to wait until you are ill. The Remedies help us cope with the ups and downs of life. They affect the emotions, which in turn affect the body. If you correct a distressing state of mind, it becomes possible to forestall a physical disturbance before it has time to manifest as illness.

ABOVE OTHER COMPLEMENTARY THERAPIES, SUCH AS AROMATHERAPY MASSAGE, CAN BE USED TO SUPPORT THE FLOWER REMEDIES.

TRAINING IN BACH FLOWER THERAPY

Dr Bach intended flower therapy to be a simple self-help measure available to people from all walks of life. Therefore, the books and leaflets available are sufficient for the home user. Seminars on flower therapy are also held regularly at the Bach Centre (*see* p.124). However, if you would like to gain a professional qualification, *see* Useful Addresses, pp.124–125. Many practitioners are qualified in some other form of therapy and employ the Bach Remedies as an adjunct to their work. If you intend to set yourself up as a Bach Flower practitioner, it would be of enormous benefit to broaden your knowledge by gaining some counselling skills and a recognized counselling qualification.

13

ABOVE COUNSELLING SKILLS ARE OF GREAT HELP TO THE BACH PRACTITIONER.

BUYING THE REMEDIES

The Stock Concentrates may be obtained from many health shops, some chemists, or by mail order (*see* Useful Addresses, pp.124–125).

HOW DO THE
REMEDIES WORK?

CHAPTER TWO

Until very recently, a non-esoteric explanation for the way the Remedies work would have appeared inconceivable. Indeed, authors have previously tended to steer clear of the harsh light of scientific reason in favour of the soft shadows of spiritual reflection. At last, however, with the wonderful awakening of science in the form of quantum physics and the development of mind/body medicine, an explanation may be possible.

THE LIFE-FORCE

Before we can begin to understand how the Remedies work, we need to move away from the materialistic bias. The doctrine of materialism holds that the body, and indeed all life, is essentially biochemical in nature and that the reality of the mind is merely a function of matter. But can we really reduce the human being to the level of chemicals? Let us consider for a moment the remarkable co-ordination and synergistic action of our physiology.

We tend to view the body as a machine composed of many parts and functions operating in separate compartments, when in fact, like the Earth's eco-systems, everything is invisibly linked. At any one time we breathe, eat, talk, think, digest our food, fight off infection, renew our cells and much more besides. Blood cells, for example, rush to the site of a wound and begin to form a clot. These cells have not travelled there by chance, they actually 'know' where to go and what to do when they arrive. Indeed, every activity within the organism is animated by an invisible and seemingly intelligent force, a force that is involved with the whole of us on all levels, not just the biochemical. In the words of physician Dr Deepak Chopra, 'Intelligence makes the difference between a house designed by an architect and a pile of bricks.' Or, to consider it another way, at death, the chemicals are still present, but something has gone.

THE SCULPTURE OR THE RIVER?

The Greek philosopher Heraclitus of Ephesus believed in a world of perpetual change, of eternal 'becoming'. He made the interesting observation, 'you cannot step into the same river twice' (because the river is constantly flowing). Likewise, far from being a solid mass, the body is in a state of constant change. The skeleton, for instance, may seem solid, yet the bones we have today were not there three months ago. Cells of the body are constantly being replaced. We make a new liver every six weeks, a new skin every month and a new stomach lining every four days. In fact, 98 per cent of the atoms in our body were not there a year ago. So, the body we can see and touch is, in reality, a stream of energy.

But what of mind? For many centuries philosophers have contemplated the nature of mind. Some have concluded that mind is a phenomenon apart from physical reality, an aspect of the immortal spirit of the individual. Others have decided that mind is merely a function of the brain – a fiction, medically speaking. Although we may never know the absolute truth, modern physics has begun to move closer towards understanding the nature of mind.

In the 1970s, a series of important discoveries began that centred on a new class of minute chemicals called neurotransmitters and

neuropeptides. These chemicals were considered revolutionary at the time because they proved that the nerves did not work electrically like a telegraph system, as had been believed, but that nerve impulses were chemical in nature.

As Dr Chopra puts it in his book *Quantum Healing*:

'The arrival of neurotransmitters on the scene makes the interaction of mind and matter far more mobile and flowing than ever before – far closer to a model of a river. They also help fill the gap that apparently separates mind and body, one of the deepest mysteries man has faced since he began to consider what he is.'

Amazingly, it appears that the non-material thought gives rise to the neurochemicals. 'To think', says Chopra, 'is to practise brain chemistry, promoting a cascade of responses throughout the body.'

Another enthralling discovery that lends credence to the reality of 'mind over matter' is that receptors for neurochemicals are to be found in other parts of the body such as the skin, and on cells in the immune system called monocytes. These 'intelligent' blood cells circulate freely throughout the body, apparently sending and receiving messages just as diverse as those in the central nervous system. This means that if, when we are happy, depressed, angry, in love or whatever, we produce brain chemicals in various parts of the body, then those parts must also be

ABOVE THE DISCOVERY OF NEUROTRANSMITTERS HAS GONE SOME WAY TOWARDS EXPLAINING HOW THE MIND MAY AFFECT THE WAY THE BODY FUNCTIONS.

happy, depressed, angry or in love. Moreover, insulin, a hormone always associated with the pancreas, is now known to be produced in the brain as well, just as brain chemicals such as transferon and CCK are produced in the stomach. Without doubt, the flowing, interrelated body/mind is a reality.

VIBRATION

A well-known mathematical formula, Bell's Theorem, formulated in 1964 by Irish physicist John Bell, holds that the reality of the universe is an interconnected whole wherein all objects and events respond to one another's changes in state. British astronomer Sir Arthur Eddington went so far as to conclude that an intelligent force holds the universe together: 'The stuff of the world is mind stuff'. More recently, theorists, such as British physicist David Bohm, have reached a similar conclusion: that there is an 'invisible field' holding all of reality together, a field that possesses the property of knowing what is happening everywhere at once. This is the quantum mechanical world, a world beyond the atom, the proton, electron and quark – all of which can be broken down into smaller particles (at least in theory) and therefore occupy space. Whatever it is that shapes the universe and bestows it with life is non-material – it takes up no space. It is believed, therefore, that the quantum, or sub-atomic world is that of energy or vibration, and it is at this point of realization that the marriage of science and mysticism takes place. Modern physics, in tune with Eastern mysticism, pictures the universe as a continuous, dancing and vibrating web of life.

EMBRACING THE WHOLE

At the quantum level, matter, from a crystal to a human being, is essentially energy or vibration. In this realm, there is no distinction between animate and inanimate, between spirit and matter. We perceive ourselves as separate from other things because different kinds of matter and energy such as water, rock and sentient life-forms vibrate at different frequencies. Mind energy, for instance, vibrates so fast that it appears to be invisible, whereas rock vibrates so slowly that we are unaware of its essential dynamism. Likewise, humans are 'deaf' to high and low frequency sounds, but this does not mean we cannot be affected by them.

In the view of German physicist Werner Heisenberg, if we set a single strand of the cosmic web in vibration we affect the whole:

> *'The world thus appears as a complicated tissue of events in which connections of different kinds alternate or overlap or combine and thereby determine the texture of the whole.'*

In the light of all this, we can now take a look at the mode of action of the Bach Flower Remedies.

HEALING VIBRATIONS

Bach believed that the flowers used for the Remedies were of a 'higher order'. Unlike medicinal herbs that vibrate at a similar frequency to that of matter, the Flower Remedies are in tune with the finer frequencies of the mind/spirit.

By flooding our energy field (*see* pp.19–20) with these higher frequencies, our whole being (the mind/body/spirit) becomes aligned with the cosmic flow, and the discordant notes of negative emotion, which slow down our vibrations and make us feel unwell, are brought into harmony.

There are many other healing methods that act on the subtle or vibrational level – for example, homeopathy, spiritual healing, colour healing, gem therapy, music therapy and aromatherapy.

THE AURA

As we have already seen, vibrational healing methods such as homeopathy and the Bach Flower Remedies act at a subtle level. Many therapists working with these remedies believe that the healing effect is triggered in the human energy field, or aura, which surrounds and interpenetrates the physical aspect. From this field, which is essentially a thought-form, the healing effect of the remedies filters 'inwards', as it were, to the physical level. In contrast, material medicines such as herbs and drugs move 'outwards' from the physical level, eventually affecting the aura.

Although psychics describe the aura differently, according to their own level of psychic perception, it is generally agreed that the aura is a rainbow emanation (some sensitives can see its colours) surrounding the body.

The aura is composed of at least three, and possibly seven, 'layers' of energy, each layer vibrating at a different frequency.

The physical body or matter vibrates at the slowest or densest frequency, while the subtle body, like electricity, vibrates much faster, which is why we are usually unaware of its existence. The part of the subtle body closest to the physical level, emanating about an inch from the body, is the etheric or vital body. This is most interesting because it

LEFT CRYSTALS WORK ON AN INDIVIDUAL'S AURIC FIELD IN THE SAME WAY AS THE BACH FLOWER REMEDIES, AND CAN BE USED AS A COMPLEMENTARY THERAPY.

vibrates at a frequency that can be detected by a high voltage technique called Kirlian photography. The information captured by this process shows a kind of luminescence and streams of energy flowing from the hands or feet. To the trained eye, these patterns reflect the emotional and physical state of the individual and can be used as a diagnostic tool.

A healthy aura is rather like a filter, allowing only that which is beneficial to affect us. The Bach Flower Remedies seek to harmonize the subtle energy frequencies within the aura, which can become weakened by the stresses and strains of life. A weakened aura will give rise to illness. In order to enhance the action of the Remedies, we can learn to control and strengthen our own aura. This is an excellent discipline because a strong aura protects us from influences of all kinds – anything from germs to stress (see chapter 7, p.105).

In His Own Words

Let us conclude this chapter with a few quotations from Bach's concise work *Heal Thyself*:

'Disease will never be cured by present materialistic methods, for the simple reason that disease in its origin is not material.'

'The next great principle is the understanding of the Unity of all things: that the Creator of all things is love, and that everything of which we are conscious is in all its infinite number of forms a manifestation of that love.'

'The Medical School of the future will not particularly interest itself in the ultimate results and products of disease ... but knowing the true cause of sickness and aware that the obvious physical results are merely secondary, it will concentrate its efforts upon bringing harmony between body, mind and soul, which results in the relief of disease.'

LEARNING TO PRESCRIBE

CHAPTER THREE

Dr Edward Bach believed strongly that physical illness is the result of disharmony between mind and spirit. In psychotherapy the spirit is often called the 'higher self' – the all-wise aspect that manifests itself in those rare and precious moments of inspiration and clarity – those moments of profound insight into the real purpose of our existence.

The higher self is aware of our true mission in life and endeavours to realize this through the mind and emotions – the personality. However, the personality is not always aware of the higher self, so we often fail to hear the promptings of our inner voice. We go through life only half awake, guided by social conditioning and our subjective responses to the life experience. As a result, according to Bach, instead of experiencing joyfulness, purposefulness, wisdom and courage, we experience disharmony. If we could act wholly in harmony with our own spirit or higher self (which itself is a part of the greater whole, embracing the rest of humanity, the planet and the Cosmos), we would fulfil our potential

ABOVE TO EXPERIENCE TRUE HEALTH AT ITS DEEPEST AND MOST SPIRITUAL LEVEL WE MUST ATTAIN HARMONY BETWEEN MIND, BODY AND SPIRIT.

and experience profound happiness. Where there is a disconnection between the higher self and the personality, there is dis-ease.

The ultimate healing potential of the Flower Remedies stems from their ability to release the energy block between the personality and the higher self. In this way, the Remedies help to bring about the necessary change in psychological and spiritual outlook, without which there can be no true healing.

Of course, the physical body is an interrelated part of the whole – the body-mind-spirit. Therefore, it is important to become aware of our needs on every level. We cannot neglect the body in favour of attaining spiritual awareness, nor pursue the path of physical/material gratification at the expense of our spiritual needs. The result would be an imbalance of energies.

PRESCRIBING FOR ONESELF

SELF-KNOWLEDGE

Before we can begin to prescribe for others, we need to achieve self-knowledge. Observe how you feel when you need a particular Remedy, and how you feel after taking it.

A common difficulty in self-diagnosis, especially when one is going through a crisis, is the inability to step back from oneself sufficiently to be able to recognize which Flowers are required.

This is where a friend or a Bach Flower practitioner can

ABOVE BEFORE YOU BEGIN TO PRESCRIBE REMEDIES FOR OTHERS, IT IS VITAL THAT YOU EXPERIENCE THEIR HEALING PROPERTIES FOR YOURSELF.

help. Talking things through with an understanding person is a necessary part of the healing process and can help us connect with our own inner strength.

RESPONSES TO TREATMENT

During the first weeks of treatment, the Flower radiations may only embrace the superficial emotions rather than the deep-rooted fears and conflicts that are causing the present physical and mental condition. However, by dealing with each new emotional state as it arises, earlier blockages will eventually work through to the surface and out of your system. When this happens you might notice a temporary worsening of physical symptoms, and experience lesser or greater crises of consciousness. However, any aggravation will only last a few days and should be taken as a positive sign that the correct Remedy has been chosen.

It should be emphasized that the intensity of the reaction appears to relate to individual sensitivity and to one's basic openness to change. The majority of people notice subtle changes over a period of weeks or months, gradually feeling more optimistic and better able to deal with the ups and downs of life. However, should you feel overwhelmed by the changes taking place within your body and mind, though this is a rare occurrence, you should discontinue use of the Flower Remedies and seek professional help from a Bach therapist or counsellor well-versed in the area of 'personal growth'.

23

FINDING THE RIGHT REMEDY

When you first read the Flower Remedy descriptions in chapter 4 (*see* pp.33–85), you may feel you need all of them! However, Bach found that the vibration of one correctly chosen Flower had a deeper and more profound effect than a composite

ABOVE IF YOU ARE UNSURE EXACTLY WHICH REMEDY IS BEST SUITED TO YOUR PARTICULAR NEEDS, SEVERAL REMEDIES MAY BE TAKEN AT ONCE. THEY ARE USUALLY MIXED WITH WATER BEFORE TAKING.

of all 38 Remedies. Nonetheless, many people may temporarily require a composite of six or more Flowers. It should not be too difficult to limit your choice to within six Remedies, but if you feel you need seven or eight, it is better to include them all than unintentionally omit one of the essential Flowers. In time, experience will help you refine the selection process. The best way to begin is to write down the Remedies you feel you need, then look at each one more closely to find out which is your basic Type Remedy and which are the Helpers.

TYPE REMEDIES

The Type Remedy is the Flower vibration that corresponds to your basic character as a whole. You may be an extrovert, a natural leader and very outspoken. This would suggest Remedies such as Vine, Vervain and Impatiens. If, on the other hand, you are quiet and reserved, then look to Remedies such as Mimulus, Centaury or Water Violet. Of course, each Flower vibration has its positive as well as its negative aspect. The positive side to the Impatiens type, for instance, is seen in those who, though quick to learn, are patient and understanding of those who are not as bright. However, when the vibrations of the Impatiens type slow down, the negative aspect of this personality comes to the fore – impatience and lack of tact with those who are not as quick on the uptake. Interestingly, Bach observed that the way a person behaves when unwell is often the key to their Type Remedy.

HELPER REMEDIES

The Helper Remedies address the superficial emotional states of mind that are not characteristic, but are temporary. For instance, you may harbour feelings of jealousy or hatred towards a former partner's new lover (Holly), or feel nervous and apprehensive before a court case (Mimulus).

On the whole, most of the 38 Remedies can act as either a Type Remedy or a Helper Remedy.

BECOMING FAMILIAR WITH THE REMEDIES

The following methods will help you to become familiar with the
Flower Remedies:

1 Try to 'prescribe' for characters in television soaps or in novels.
Fictional characters are usually exaggerated versions
of real people, and so display quite definite
personality traits. Or practise diagnosing
Type Remedies for people in the public eye –
politicians, members of the Royal
Family or TV personalities, for
example. Also, observe your own family,
friends and neighbours.

2 Look back over your life and identify
the emotional states that predominated at
different stages. How did you feel on
your first day at school, for instance?
Were you happy and self-assured, the
dominant child within the group
(Vine)? Or did you feel intimidated by
the exuberance of the other children
and therefore too shy to join in
(Mimulus)? What about your love life? Were you always the
rejected partner, the over-possessive lover who stifled the joy
and spontaneity out of every relationship (Chicory)? Or have
you always been the victim, the willing slave to a stronger, more
forceful personality (Centaury)?

3 Now think of the present. Consider how you respond to
criticism; how you might react if you were short-changed at the
supermarket; how you deal with illness and pain. By observing
your reactions to the life experience, you will soon determine the
correct Type Remedy.

ABOVE THE BRIGHT BLUE
FLOWERS OF THE CHICORY
PLANT ARE USED TO MAKE
A REMEDY TO HELP US TO
LOVE SPONTANEOUSLY.

25

DREAMWORK

Though not a traditional way of working with the Flower Remedies, in my own experience Dreamwork is an invaluable tool in Bach therapy. Most dreams represent situations and patterns needing resolution – that is, they pose questions and invite responses. Concentrate on the feelings and responses, or lack of response, your dreams evoke in you, and prescribe accordingly. For example, you may be shocked by an expression of jealousy and violence in a dream (Holly), or by some other equally powerful reaction rarely expressed in the non-dreaming state.

The Flower Remedies tend to activate the dream life, which is why it is useful to keep a record of your dreams for about a month whilst taking the Remedies. Once you can identify recurring themes and emotions, you will be in a good position to begin deeper work with the Remedies. In fact, you can even ask for a significant dream just before falling asleep; the sub-conscious will usually oblige.

Keep a pen and notebook beside the bed, and immediately on waking (for dreams fade very quickly) write down all you can remember about a significant dream. If the memory of a dream does evade you, record the particular emotion or mood it may have evoked. Then, try to answer the following questions that are based on the work of dream therapist Strephon Kaplan-Williams:

ABOVE WRITE DOWN YOUR DREAMS AS SOON AS YOU WAKE. DREAMWORK CAN BE A USEFUL TOOL IN HELPING YOU TO MATCH A REMEDY WITH YOUR PARTICULAR NEEDS.

1 What am I doing and why am I doing it?
2 What do I most need to deal with in this dream?
3 Would I react this way in waking life, or am I reacting in a very different way?
4 What in this particular dream is related to things in other dreams I have had?

5 What in this dream is related to what is going on in me or in my life at present?
6 Why did I have this dream? What am I needing to look at, or make a choice about?

PRESCRIBING FOR OTHERS

Once you have worked with the Remedies for a while and can prescribe for yourself, you should be able to prescribe for your family and friends.

THE CONSULTATION

A good therapist is a person who has developed two essential skills – the ability to empathize and the capacity to listen. The feeling of empathy is one that is closely linked with our intuitive self, whereas sympathy hooks into our personal distress, thereby draining our emotional energy. So, prior to the consultation, you will find it helpful to spend a few minutes concentrating on becoming centred and connected with your higher self (*see* chapter 7).

ABOVE DIAGNOSING FOR A STRANGER REQUIRES MORE SKILL THAN SELF-DIAGNOSIS. EMPATHY AND INTUITION ARE THE ESSENTIAL QUALITIES OF A GOOD THERAPIST.

To listen as a therapist is to hear on various levels. We listen with the intellect to the words that a patient uses and the way their story is expressed. For instance, 'I've tried everything, but what's the use' (Gorse). Or, 'I know it's all my fault, I should have been more understanding' (Pine). Do they speak in a low and anxious voice (Mimulus)? Or do they lean forward, clasp your arm and swamp you with their life story (Heather)?

We should also listen with our eyes, observing their body language. Are they relaxed and self-assured, sitting back comfortably in the chair? Or, by contrast, are they perched on the edge, drumming their fingers on the table?

Above all, we should listen with our intuition – our higher self. Perhaps there is something in their eyes that speaks of grief, anger, bitterness or fear – even though at this stage they may not have acknowledged the harbouring of such feelings.

If the person finds it difficult to express their emotional outlook, gently guide them in the right direction by asking about their childhood, occupation, home life and so forth. Try to establish how they react to the life experience. For instance, if they mention bereavement, divorce or a broken love affair, try to discover how they coped at the time. Did they resort to alcohol, overeating, drugs? What situations do they fear at present – an imminent operation, childbirth, a change of job, retirement?

Sometimes the effects of shock can be so delayed that years might pass before any sign becomes apparent – perhaps in the guise of depression, guilt or fear. The trauma of abortion, a car crash or the death of a loved one may lie at the root of a person's present physical and emotional state. In such circumstances always prescribe Star of Bethlehem for the shock, and other Remedies to help the depression, fear, guilt, or whatever it might be.

As the person talks, jot down all the Remedies that come to mind. However, try not to let note-taking become too obtrusive. It is important to maintain a relaxed and equal relationship, an atmosphere of trust, throughout the consultation. You can always make notes immediately afterwards while the person's story is still fresh in your mind.

When discussing the Flower Remedies with the person always dwell on the positive qualities or virtues to be achieved by them. For instance, instead of emphasizing that Gentian is for their 'doubting Thomas' attitude, let them go away with the knowledge that Gentian will help them develop the certainty that their problems can be overcome.

My own approach is usually to include some 'homework' such as visualization, breathing exercises, a relaxation tape or slow stretching movements to release physical and emotional tension. If there is a great deal of self-disgust I suggest ways of nurturing the self. This might include a daily aromatic bath with a few drops of Crab Apple added to the aromatherapy oils or something simple such as buying themselves a small present once in a while.

ABOVE BREATHING EXERCISES ARE A USEFUL ADJUNCT TO FLOWER REMEDIES. THEY HELP TO RELAX BOTH THE BODY AND THE MIND.

29

SPECIAL USES FOR FLOWER REMEDIES

PREGNANCY

Flower Remedies are perfectly safe and highly beneficial to the expectant mother and her unborn child. The method of diagnosis and treatment is no different from usual. The Remedies can be of help where there is apprehension or emotional suffering during the pre- and post-natal periods.

Many practitioners suggest a basic composite of Rescue Remedy (a composite of five Bach Flower Remedies – *see* p.85) and Walnut. This mixture can be taken a few days before the expected date of delivery, during labour and for about a month afterwards to help both mother and child cope with reaction and change.

Remedies can also be used in the following cases: Mimulus for fear of childbirth (or in extreme cases, Rock Rose); Impatiens to help those who become irritable and impatient as they near term; Oak, Hornbeam, and Olive may be indicated if the woman is exhausted during labour and feels she can no longer carry on; Mustard, Gorse, Gentian, Sweet Chestnut or Willow may uplift the spirits of the mother suffering from 'baby blues' during the post-natal period. Incidentally, there are many recorded cases of mothers having experienced an easy and gentle birth and a rapid recovery as a result of taking Rescue Remedy shortly before parturition.

ABOVE PREGNANT WOMEN CAN TAKE THE REMEDIES IN THE KNOWLEDGE THAT THEY HAVE NO TOXIC SIDE-EFFECTS AND WILL NOT HARM THEIR UNBORN CHILD.

BABIES

You might be surprised to learn that newborn babies are relatively easy to diagnose, even though they are unable to tell us about their state of mind. For example: the Agrimony baby is usually happy and gurgling and is very little trouble – unless there is something definitely wrong; the Chicory baby is very demanding and hates to be alone; the Clematis baby, on the other hand, shows very little interest in anything, sleeps a great deal and sometimes has to be woken up for feeds; the Mimulus baby is very nervous, frightened by loud noises and sudden movements; while the Impatiens baby has quite a temper.

ABOVE FLOWER REMEDIES ARE SAFE FOR BABIES AND CAN BE ADDED TO BOTTLED WATER. IF THE BABY IS BREAST FED, HOWEVER, THE MOTHER MAY TAKE THE REMEDY.

Bach believed that by addressing the baby's type or personality difficulty, the passing moods or negative states of mind would be easily transmuted, before they began to take root. When a spirit can be helped at this stage, its passage through life will be much easier and happier for the personality. The dosage for babies is the same as for adults, though nursing mothers can take the Remedy instead (*see* p.85).

CHILDREN

Children are a joy for the Bach Flower practitioner for they often respond rapidly and extremely well to the Remedies. This is because the child tends to express his or her feelings openly – that is, until the self-conscious phase of adolescence.

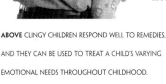

First, try to establish the child's Type Remedy if you can. This will be required at intervals throughout childhood, and indeed into maturity, in case the personality changes radically (not an unknown phenomenon). Then establish which other Remedies will be supportive. For example, Walnut, the Remedy for change or transition, is most helpful during the turbulence of puberty. Vine will help transmute the aggressive energy of the school bully into positive qualities of leadership. Centaury, by contrast, will help the bully's victim! Holly will embrace the child who is jealous of her baby brother, while Rock Rose or Rescue Remedy will dispel her nightmares. If the child's disturbing dreams are caused by a recurrent upsetting memory, then Honeysuckle is indicated. For fear of the dark, consider Mimulus. For vague fears of unknown origin, especially if accompanied by sweating and trembling, turn to Aspen. For the wakeful, highly active child choose

31

ABOVE CLINGY CHILDREN RESPOND WELL TO REMEDIES, AND THEY CAN BE USED TO TREAT A CHILD'S VARYING EMOTIONAL NEEDS THROUGHOUT CHILDHOOD.

Vervain. And for the drowsy, apathetic child, prescribe Clematis. Finally, not forgetting the long-suffering, over-anxious parent, Red Chestnut will engender a sense of calm and positivity.

ANIMALS

As verified by numerous veterinary case studies, animals tend to respond to the Flower Remedies even more rapidly, and sometimes more profoundly, than humans.

The diagnosis is made in the usual way, though one must try to empathize with the animal in order to perceive its state of mind. The nervous animal, for instance, who tends to jump with fright at the slightest sound or any sudden movement, needs Mimulus. The over-possessive dog who drives his owner berserk by being constantly at her heels could do with a dose of Chicory. The jealous, possessive dog who barks at everyone should be prescribed Holly. The cat with nine lives who has been hit by a car on more than one occasion needs Chestnut Bud to enable it to learn from past experiences, and so on.

ABOVE A NERVOUS CAT CAN BE TREATED WITH MIMULUS. THE CAT WHO NEEDS TO LEARN FROM PAST MISTAKES SHOULD BE PRESCRIBED CHESTNUT BUD.

32

George MacLeod, one of the world's foremost authorities on the use of homeopathic remedies for animals, encourages all his fellow veterinarians to use the Rescue Remedy for shock, accidents, injuries, pre-surgical work, and so forth. 'Dr Bach was a medical genius', MacLeod says.

PLANTS

Even plants can respond to the Flower Remedies. For example, Rescue Remedy is indispensable (followed by Walnut and Crab Apple) when plants are suffering from pest damage or when they are being transplanted (*see* p.88).

THE 38 HEALERS

CHAPTER FOUR

The 38 Flower Remedies appear here in alphabetical order by common name. As well as a brief botanical introduction and method of potentization, each remedy profile contains its key negative state of mind. This is a summary of the key personality traits that can be helped by a particular Remedy. A more detailed account follows to confirm whether or not you have chosen the correct Remedy.

The positive potential following treatment describes what occurs when the positive aspects within the psyche are brought to the fore, freed from the chains of fear, doubt, anger and uncertainty.

Other self-help measures such as yoga, nature attunement, positive affirmations, visualization, meditation and so on, are suggested where appropriate because they encourage a full and active participation in our own healing – a very important tenet of holistic therapy.

ABOVE YOGA IS A RELAXING SELF-HELP TECHNIQUE THAT COMBINES WELL WITH SOME OF THE REMEDIES.

Sometimes it can be difficult to decide between two similar Remedies, so where this occurs, a comparison has been drawn to help clarify the matter.

A brief description of the child Type is also included at the end of each section.

Finally, the Rescue Remedy is discussed on p.85. This is a first-aid Remedy that combines Rock Rose, Clematis, Impatiens, Cherry Plum and Star of Bethlehem.

CHARACTER TYPES

Dr Bach grouped the Remedies under seven headings:

1 For those who have fear: Rock Rose, Mimulus, Cherry Plum, Aspen, Red Chestnut.

2 For those who suffer uncertainty: Cerato, Scleranthus, Gentian, Gorse, Hornbeam, Wild Oat.

3 For insufficient interest in present circumstances: Clematis, Honeysuckle, Wild Rose, Olive, White Chestnut, Mustard, Chestnut Bud.

4 For loneliness: Water Violet, Impatiens, Heather.

5 For those over-sensitive to influences and ideas: Agrimony, Centaury, Walnut, Holly.

6 For despondency and despair: Larch, Pine, Elm, Sweet Chestnut, Star of Bethlehem, Willow, Oak, Crab Apple.

7 For over-care for the welfare of others: Chicory, Vervain, Vine, Beech, Rock Water.

AGRIMONY (*Agrimonia eupatoria*)

A softly hairy plant with spikes of faintly fragrant yellow flowers. Grows to a height of 30–60cm. Widespread and common in grassy places. Flowers June–August.

Method of potentization: Sun.

Key negative state: Mental torture concealed behind a happy-go-lucky facade.

The Agrimony type is easy to recognize. He is the life and soul of any party – the exuberant yet kindly jester who would never make fun of another, for he laughs only at himself. However, Agrimony wears the actor's mask of Comedy and Tragedy. The joyful public persona is very different from the creased face of woe that hides in the closet. Rarely will the true Agrimony soul seek help of his own volition. He prefers to go on pretending to the world, and often to himself, that life is just wonderful. When alone (a situation he tries to avoid at all costs) he attempts to stifle the worrying thoughts that bombard his consciousness, but with very little success. Often he has trouble sleeping and may even resort to alcohol or drugs as an escape from his problems.

Only the one he loves and trusts the most will ever be allowed to glimpse the truth – and it is this person who will encourage and, with luck, eventually persuade him to seek the help he so desperately needs.

Positive potential following treatment: The ability truly to laugh at life because personal problems will be viewed from a more balanced perspective – that of the genuine optimist who possesses an innate talent for creating harmony where there is discord.

Other self-help measures: Relaxation, yoga or Tai Chi. Where there is a drink or drugs related problem, seek expert help.

The Agrimony child: This child appears outwardly cheerful but, as his mother or closest carer knows, he suffers inwardly. Great importance is attached to the impression he is making on his friends, family and teachers.

ASPEN (*Populus tremula*)
A small tree, up to about 15m, related to the great black poplar. Found throughout Britain on poor soils and in damp woodland. Flowers February–April.
Method of potentization: Boiling.
Key negative state: Inexplicable fears stemming from the psyche; nightmares; fear of some impending evil.
Comparison: With Mimulus, whose fear is of known or worldly origin (e.g. fear of an impending court case).

35

The Aspen type, like the delicate tree itself, trembles in the slightest breeze. She is hypersensitive to 'bad vibes' of any nature, be it the eerie atmosphere of a building or the unpleasant undertones sometimes generated within groups of people. She will also be disturbed by the 'sinister shadows' surrounding certain individuals whom she suspects of being mentally unbalanced in some way; or she may awaken in the night, trembling and sweating, terrified by the notion that something evil lurks behind the wardrobe. Although it is said that Aspen's fears are of the mind, this does not necessarily mean that they are a mere fantasy. Aspen may be very psychic but, instead of tuning into the joyous events of life, she tends to focus on catastrophe – an impending plane crash or a bomb explosion, for instance.

Positive potential following treatment: Fearlessness in the knowledge that one's Guardian is the universal power of Love.

Other self-help measures: Auric control (*see* p.105). Regular practice of this technique will serve as a mode of psychic protection, a filter against harmful thoughts and influences of any nature. Most importantly, it will allow much more control over what comes through.

Choose activities that are 'grounding' such as gardening, walking, sport, cooking, receiving or giving massage – or even watching a funny film or play. Avoid anything that will disturb the mind, such as horror films or books, and intoxicants such as alcohol or cannabis. It may also be wise to avoid any conscious form of psychic development such as occult practice or even yoga, unless under the guidance of an experienced tutor.

ABOVE GARDENING IS A GROUNDING ACTIVITY THAT WILL HELP DISPEL ASPEN'S FEAR OF THE UNKNOWN.

The Aspen child: This child suffers from recurring nightmares and may even sleepwalk. Very often demands that a light be left on all night.

BEECH (*Fagus sylvatica*)

A majestic tree widespread throughout Britain, growing to a height of 30–40m. Male and female flowers appear on the same plant forming a purplish brown tassel on a long stalk. Blooms April–May.

Method of potentization: Boiling.

Key negative state: Intolerance of others, criticism and arrogance.

Comparisons: Compare with Vine whose need is to dominate, and with Vervain, the forceful fanatic whose need is to convert.

ABOVE THE LEAVES OF THE BEECH TREE ARE USED TO MAKE A REMEDY FOR INTOLERANCE.

37

The Beech personality perceives little that is good or beautiful in the world. He has few friends in the world because his over-critical and intolerant personality irritates others beyond measure. He sees no virtue in the diversity of human nature, his motto being: 'Why can't they do as I do?'

Beech often fails to recognize the fact that not everyone is born with the same gifts or has the same social or cultural background. Even the small habits, gestures and mannerisms of others are annoying to Beech.

Sadly, his own life may have been one of hard-swallowed hatred, humiliation and disappointment. This bitterness, which often manifests as digestive upsets, is projected on to the outside world, for Beech has yet to reach his innermost feelings. As a result of this suppression, Beech finds it impossible to enter into the feelings of other people.

Positive potential following treatment: Tolerance and understanding of the difficulties of others; the ability to see the good in everyone and everything.

Other self-help measures: When criticizing others, notice whether they are generalized criticisms such as 'He's stupid' or 'She's a bore'. If so, change generalized criticism to specific descriptions of behaviour so that 'She's a fool' becomes 'She giggles when nervous' or 'She's too loud', for example. Begin to look for the positive qualities in people. This counteracts the tendency to see everything and everyone in negative terms. Commune with nature as often as possible.

Take up some form of physical activity that counteracts rigidity of body and mind, for example, dancing, yoga, Tai Chi and so on. Seek some frivolity in life!

The Beech child: He may be reflecting parental attitudes (consider this deeply), or perhaps he is feeling belittled by an elder, more dominant or popular sibling.

ABOVE EXERCISE SUCH AS TAI CHI WILL HELP THE BEECH TYPE TO BECOME MORE FLEXIBLE IN BOTH BODY AND MIND.

CENTAURY (*Centaurium erythraea*)

A variable annual, 5–35cm tall (depending on its habitat). Widespread and common in poor, dry, grassy places and on dunes. The small rose-pink, star-like flowers open only in bright sunshine. Blooms June–August.

Method of potentization: Sun.

Key negative state: Lack of will-power to refuse the demands of other people, therefore becoming a willing slave.

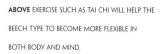

ABOVE CENTAURY IS A TRADITIONAL MEDICINAL PLANT WITH BRIGHT PINK FLOWERS THAT GROWS IN CHALKY SOIL.

Centaury believes she was born to serve. She is a martyr who suppresses her own needs simply to keep the peace and to gain favour in the eyes of another.

Centaury may even forgo marriage and a family of her own in order to care for an ageing parent or relative. Often she is tired, sometimes completely drained by the incessant demands of other people, yet she rarely complains for she is resigned to drudgery.

Unfortunately, Centaury misses out on many things in life, particularly the joy and excitement that independence and a sense of adventure often bring.

Should she marry, the chances are that she will attract a tyrant for a partner. It has been said that Centaury connects with a stronger personality in order to evade the process of growing up, which would involve making her own decisions.

Positive potential following treatment: To know when to give of oneself and when to withhold – the ability to mix with others while preserving one's own identity; to live one's life according to one's own true mission.

Other self-help measures: Martial arts such as judo, which will help to cultivate inner strength, poise and self-confidence; assertiveness training. Practise the aura strengthening visualization (*see* p.105).

The Centaury child: She is quiet, sensitive, responsive – hardly any trouble, but she may be the prey of the school bully.

RIGHT THE CENTAURY TYPE OFTEN SUFFERS FROM DEEP EXHAUSTION DUE TO HER WILLINGNESS TO ACT AS A SLAVE FOR OTHERS.

CERATO (*Ceratostigma willmottianum*)
The only cultivated plant used in the Bach system, Cerato is a flowering shrub from the Himalayas, about 60cm in height. The beautiful bright blue flowers open in August and September.

Method of potentization: Sun.

Key negative state: Insufficient confidence in themselves to make their own decisions.

Comparison: Scleranthus is torn between two things, but unlike Cerato, rarely bothers others with the trivia of day to day decision-making. Scleranthus eventually struggles to find the answer from within.

ABOVE NATIVE TO THE HIMALAYAS, CERATO IS THE ONLY CULTIVATED PLANT IN THE BACH PHARMACOPOEIA. ITS BLUE FLOWERS APPEAR IN LATE SUMMER.

40

Cerato is plagued with uncertainty. Even though he is intuitive and possesses sound judgement, he rarely trusts the promptings of his inner voice, and thus cannot act on his own volition. Instead, Cerato drives his family and friends to distraction with his incessant demands for advice or confirmation of the wisdom of every single move he makes.

Not only is Cerato easily swayed by the opinions of others, but he has also been known to imitate the style of dress and even the gestures and mannerisms of the one he most admires which can, of course, make him appear foolish at times.

He will experience the occasional moment of clarity in which he will pour out his most frequent lament, 'I knew I should have done that. Now it's too late!' Or, having drained the energy of just about everyone in his vicinity, he will infuriatingly decide to do it his own way after all!

Positive potential following treatment: To trust one's own ability to judge between right and wrong – to act and remain uninfluenced by any advice to the contrary.

Other self-help measures: Visualization. Concentrate on the idea of making contact with your higher self. Then, in your mind's eye, see yourself making an important decision and acting on it. Dreamwork (*see* pp.26–27) can also be useful.

The Cerato child: This state of mind is more likely to emerge during adolescence. Cerato constantly seeks the approval of others (particularly his peers) and insists on wearing the most fashionable clothes, whether they suit him or not! If he is attached to a truly 'bad crowd' of friends then Cerato combined with Walnut will help him to sever the links.

CHERRY PLUM (*Prunus cerasifera*)

A small thornless tree growing to a height of 6–8m. The flowers are pure white. Common as a hedgerow shrub, mainly in the south of England. Flowers from late February to early April.

Method of potentization: Boiling.

41

Key negative state: Fear of losing one's mind; uncontrolled outbreaks of temper or hysteria.

Cherry Plum harbours a morbid fear that she lives on borrowed time. She feels that at any moment she may lose her grip on reality.

There is also the terrible impulse to harm other people or herself. Thoughts of suicide wash in and out of her mind like some menacing black tide.

But how did she reach such a state of desperation? She may have suffered a prolonged period of anxiety or grief and now finds herself on the verge of a nervous breakdown.

ABOVE THE CHERRY PLUM TYPE IS A PICTURE OF DEEP DESPAIR AND MAY HAVE SUICIDAL TENDENCIES. THE REMEDY IS NEEDED TO RESTORE CONFIDENCE AND GIVE MENTAL STRENGTH.

Or for many years she may have dealt with the trials and tribulations of life in an outwardly controlled and 'dignified' manner. But the turbulence of unexpressed emotion causes great pressure and distortion; destructive images and forces eventually thrust their way to the surface. Cherry Plum is no longer able to hold back, and the volcano erupts! However, with the right kind of emotional support, no serious damage will ensue, for that exploding volcano is her psychic safety valve.

Cherry Plum is included in the Rescue Remedy (*see* p.85) for violent outbursts and hysteria.

Positive potential following treatment: The ability to handle great inner forces spontaneously and with a true sense of calm, for the distress is healed by the balancing forces of the spirit or higher self.

Other self-help measures: If feeling suicidal, seek expert help – phone the Samaritans and/or contact your doctor. Find out about psychotherapy, especially if Cherry Plum is your Type Remedy.

Instead of turning aggressive energy inwards, learn to harness it, using its dynamism to give more steam to any project or activity.

The Cherry Plum child: There may be sudden uncontrolled outbreaks of rage, especially when the child throws herself on the ground or hits her head against the wall – the typical uncontrollable temper tantrum.

CHESTNUT BUD (*Aesculus hippocastanum*)

The Horse Chestnut tree was brought to Britain from Turkey in the early 17th century. Only the sticky buds are used for this Remedy, the flowers being used for White Chestnut essence. The buds are picked in early April.

Method of potentization: Boiling.

Key negative state: Failure to learn by experience; need for repetition.

Chestnut Bud experiences déjà vu more than most. However, instead of being a rather pleasant or intriguing experience, it tends to lead to the feeling, 'Oh no, not again!' Over and over again Chestnut Bud makes the same mistakes, failing to learn from past experiences.

Why does Chestnut Bud constantly come up against the same stumbling blocks? The reason may be indifference, too much haste or lack of observation. In a sense, he is a young spirit flowing against the tide of life. In his naivety, he fails to learn life's most fundamental lesson – that we cannot escape from the past into the future, for the future reflects the past, even though our real development is taking place in the present, in the eternal NOW.

Positive potential following treatment: The ability to keep one's attention in the present; to gain knowledge and wisdom from every experience.

Other self-help measures: In a state of deep relaxation (*see* pp.103–104), or just before falling asleep, ask yourself, 'Why do I keep hitting the same barrier? What am I supposed to be learning from this experience?' Then ask: 'What changes do I need to make in order to progress?' Practise this daily until you receive insight. The answers may come in various ways – perhaps in a moment of inspiration during or immediately after the exercise. Or the message might come more slowly and in a subtle way, so that after a while you realize that your outlook has become clear even though the actual moment of insight cannot be pinpointed. The answers may even reach you through a dream or, more curiously, through synchronicity; that is to say, through some element in the environment that you

43

ABOVE AS YOU RELAX IN BED, QUESTION WHY YOU FAIL TO LEARN FROM PAST MISTAKES. EVENTUALLY THE ANSWER WILL COME TO YOU.

perceive as meaningful. It could be a phrase read at random in a book, an event that changes your usual routine, the title of a film, or the words of a friend, and so on. Indeed the answer may be blowing in the wind – if you are able to catch it.

The Chestnut Bud child: This child finds it difficult to pay attention; he is a slow learner. He will keep forgetting things. In spite of being reminded, he will keep forgetting his P.E. kit or his pencil case, for instance.

CHICORY (*Cichorium intybus*)

A perennial herb up to 1m in height, common on chalky soil. Grows on wasteland and on the edges of fields and roadsides. The pretty blue flowers open from July to September, but last only a day, fading as soon as they are picked.

Method of potentization: Sun.

Key negative state: Possessiveness; selfishness, self-pity.

Chicory cannot express unconditional love, for the love aspect is hindered in its outward flow, and is turned inward to the self. Chicory demands sympathy and appreciation from others, yet rarely can she give as much in return, or if she does, there is always a price to pay.

If she does not receive the love and affection she believes is her due, she will become manipulative and deceitful, engendering a sense of guilt in those susceptible to emotional blackmail.

LEFT AROMATHERAPY MAY MAKE THE CHICORY TYPE FEEL LOVED AND NOURISHED.

As a parent, Chicory is inclined to be possessive and overprotective, causing her children to feel stifled. She is compelled to control – organizing, criticizing, and generally frog-marching her loved ones through life. And of course, she suffers deep resentment when they later rebel.

Sadly, Chicory may have had a loveless childhood. She feels a deep inner emptiness and lack of fulfilment, so craves recognition and affection. But her need is a bottomless pit that can never be filled.

Positive potential following treatment: The ability to give without demanding anything in return; to be secure in oneself.

Other self-help measures: If the problem is deep-rooted rather than a temporary state of mind, it would be helpful to seek counselling, or a nurturing therapy such as aromatherapy.

Commune with nature whenever you can. Find inner peace by practising deep relaxation, breathing and meditation exercises (*see* chapter 7).

Begin to change negative thought-patterning by repeating the following affirmation just before you fall asleep at night: 'I am finding security within myself. I allow joy to flow through my mind and body and out to others.'

The Chicory child: This child demands a great deal of attention; she cannot bear to be alone, and may even feign illness to get her own way and the attention of others.

45

CLEMATIS (*Clematis vitalba*)

A woody climber found in hedgerows and woodland, especially on chalk and limestone soils in the south of Britain and much of Ireland. The trusses of faintly fragrant, greenish-white flowers appear from July to September. The plant is also commonly known as Old Man's Beard because the styles develop into woolly greyish-white plumes in the autumn.

Method of potentization: Sun.

Key negative state: Day-dreaming; indifference; little attention in the present; a bemused state of mind; unconsciousness.

Clematis is not of this world. His faraway look and lack of vitality is indicative of one who dwells in the realm of fantasy and dreams. He has little or no interest in the present, for his thoughts are far away in the future, in happier times to come.

It has been said of Clematis that he hears without listening and sees without looking, so forgets most of what is said to him. He also likes to sleep, not just at bedtime, but on the bus, at a lecture, in front of the television, in fact almost anywhere and at any time. With his life energies diverted inwards in this way, he never becomes angry or violent, deeply depressed, nor even joyful. Good news is greeted with as much indifference as bad.

In illness, Clematis makes little or no effort to get better, and may even welcome the prospect of death in the hope of meeting on the spirit plane some beloved one whom he has lost. This extreme lack of effort to get well prompted Bach to call the Clematis state of mind 'a polite form of suicide'.

Incidentally, the Clematis state may also be of a passing nature, where there is unconsciousness, fainting or any bemused state of mind brought about by shock. For this reason, Clematis is included in the Rescue Remedy (*see* p.85).

Positive potential following treatment: If creative, as most Clematis types are, the ability to bring into realization one's creative inspiration. To take a lively interest in all things because the purpose of life can be fully appreciated.

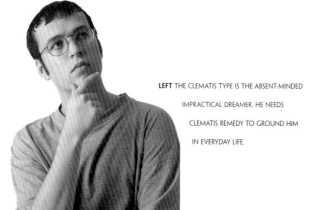

LEFT THE CLEMATIS TYPE IS THE ABSENT-MINDED IMPRACTICAL DREAMER. HE NEEDS CLEMATIS REMEDY TO GROUND HIM IN EVERYDAY LIFE.

Other self-help measures: Choose activities that are 'grounding' such as gardening, receiving or giving massage, cooking, watching a funny play or film.

Find an outlet for creativity such as painting, writing, flower arranging and so on.

Psychic ability may be present, but undisciplined esoteric work of any nature may trigger certain psychological problems, so do seek the advice of a reputable teacher or healer.

The Clematis child: He is pale and sleepy, inattentive and absent-minded. He has a poor body image and tends to bump into things. His eyes are usually unfocused, and he has a dreamy expression.

CRAB APPLE (*Malus pumila* or *sylvestris*)

The true wild apple is a small deciduous tree with a crooked trunk, fissured and cracked. It is found in hedgerows, thickets and woodland, and reaches a maximum height of 10m. The clusters of pinkish-white blossom appear in May.

Method of potentization: Boiling.

Key negative state: A feeling of being unclean; self-disgust; over-emphasis on trivial detail.

Crab Apple is filled with a sense of self-disgust. She feels somehow unclean in mind and body. Crab Apple might have a minor skin blemish such as a pimple on her chin that she examines closely in a magnifying mirror, and she then imagines that everyone else can clearly see the festering pustule in all its hideous magnitude!

In the same vein, she may be revolted by bodily functions such as breastfeeding, sex, and illness.

Her tendency to home in on detail, to magnify things under the lens of her own limited viewpoint, also spills over into other areas of her life. It may be, for instance, that the puppy has left dirty marks on the freshly washed kitchen floor, but the more important fact that the animal has injured its leg only sinks in once the floor has been rewashed and returned to its former pristine condition.

47

ABOVE TO GET RID OF FEELINGS OF SELF-DISGUST AND PHYSICAL OBSESSIVENESS, BUY YOURSELF FLOWERS ONCE A DAY FOR A WEEK.

48

Note: Crab Apple is also particularly valuable as an external treatment (*see* p.87).

Positive potential following treatment: The wisdom to see life in its proper perspective; the development of self-respect.

Other self-help measures: Aura strengthening visualization (*see* p. 105) is appropriate.

Look after yourself and indulge in self-nurturing activities such as a daily or weekly aromatic bath containing 5 drops of a favourite essential oil. Also add 5 drops of Crab Apple to the bath water.

Buy yourself a small present once a day for a week – a few flowers, an appealing picture card, an exotic fruit, and so on.

For very deep-rooted problems, do seek professional counselling or psychotherapy.

The Crab Apple child: This child is very sensitive; disgusted by such things as insects or worms, eating food from others' plates or getting dirty. The Remedy is useful during puberty, for girls who find menstruation distasteful, or for the youngster who is embarrassed by a spotty skin.

ELM (*Ulmus procera*)

Although Dutch Elm disease has destroyed most of the mature trees in Britain, many young trees appear to be thriving. A few mature specimens can still be found in some northern counties and in a few isolated nature reserves. Elm flowers are small and reddish brown, appearing in clusters in February and March, before the leaves unfurl.

Method of potentization: Boiling.

Key negative state: Temporary feelings of inadequacy, even though fulfilling one's mission in life.

Comparisons: Compare with the Hornbeam type whose fatigue is through dislike for the work he is doing, while Olive is worn out by long and continued stress. The Elm exhaustion by contrast is a temporary state.

The Elm person may be succeeding in life, following his own true mission, but he sometimes experiences despondency. He suddenly feels he has taken on more responsibility than he can carry, and fears that failure is waiting just around the corner.

He usually holds a position of importance, and is a person upon whom others rely. Indeed, everyone holds him in high esteem, for he is hardworking, capable, and reliable. However, Elm is sometimes too altruistic for his own good. He forgets that he has physical and emotional limits. Sudden exhaustion and crisis are the body/mind's cry for rest and moderation in all things. At such times, and indeed as a regular practice, he needs to find a quiet space from which problems can be viewed in perspective, thus restoring his confidence, which has been temporarily lost.

Positive potential following treatment: The ability to see problems in their proper perspective; an inner conviction that help will always come at the right moment.

Other self-help measures: Take regular walks in the countryside or in the park; allow yourself plenty of opportunity for breaks – including that all-important holiday now and again.

Treat yourself to an aromatherapy massage.

ABOVE ELM IS FOR THOSE WHO FEEL TEMPORARILY OVERWHELMED BY TAKING ON TOO MUCH RESPONSIBILITY. THE REMEDY WILL HELP TO RESTORE SELF-CONFIDENCE.

49

The Elm child: Elm is a state of mind not normally associated with young children, though the Remedy may be of use for youngsters suffering from overload at examination time.

GENTIAN (*Gentianella amarella* – Felwort)

A hairless biennial, 15–20cm in height. Found on dry, chalky or limestone soils, on hills and dunes. The flowers are purple/violet but not blue, nor spotted as in other varieties of Gentian. Blooms only in autumn, from late August to early October.

Method of potentization: Sun.

Key negative state: Being easily discouraged: scepticism and lack of faith – a 'doubting Thomas'.

Comparisons: Gentian is the first stage of hopelessness before despondency sets in – the 'two-steps-forward-one-back' feeling. The second stage is Gorse when one feels that nothing is going to help us get well. Finally, there is Sweet Chestnut, where there is nothing but oblivion ahead, and utter despair.

Gentian suffers from a deeply negative outlook. It has been said that 'she wouldn't be happy if she was happy.' She is the eternal pessimist. Gentian fails to see that her own negative outlook actually colours and shapes the course of her life, attracting the very conditions that she dreads the most.

As a temporary state of mind, Gentian is for those who suffer a setback during convalescence, for instance, or have doubts about the efficacy of the treatment being given. Their depression is from a known cause, from delay or hindrance – the negativity that breeds a sense of failure.

Positive potential following treatment: To acquire perseverance; the faith of a positive sceptic – one who sees difficulties, but does not fall into a deep gloom over them. The

ABOVE THE GENTIAN TYPE IS EASILY DISHEARTENED AND HAS A NEGATIVE OUTLOOK ON LIFE. THE GENTIAN REMEDY IS FOR THOSE WHO DOUBT.

realization that there is no failure when one is doing one's best, whatever the apparent result.

Other self-help measures: Just before you fall asleep at night say the following words: 'There is no failure when I am doing my best.'

The Gentian child: Discouraged by her schoolwork, for instance, she does not want to go back to school; or she may be the child who is torn in two as a result of being dragged back and forth between divorced parents.

GORSE (*Ulex europaeus*)

A spiny evergreen bush or shrub. Widespread in rough grassy places, especially heaths and downs. The bright yellow, almond-scented flowers appear from February onwards, though they are most abundant in April and May.

Method of potentization: Sun.

51

Key negative state: Hopelessness, negativity and despair.

Comparison: Compare with Wild Rose who is even more passive and apathetic and is unable to muster the enthusiasm to try again. The gorse type can be persuaded to try another approach.

The Gorse type suffers from the hopelessness of one who has been told 'nothing more can be done to help you'. Believing that fate has decreed suffering as his lot, he makes little mental effort to improve his situation. Yet his inner voice of wisdom may still be heard faintly beyond the din of despair. At odd moments he may even glimpse the

ABOVE GORSE IS A HARDY SHRUB THAT GROWS ON HEATHS AND DOWNLAND. IT HAS NEEDLE-LIKE LEAVES AND SCENTED YELLOW FLOWERS.

light shining through the hazy glass partition that separates his personality from its source – the higher self. At such times, unlike Wild Rose, he can be persuaded by his loved ones to try again, albeit in a half-hearted manner.

His life's lesson is to open up to the possibility that the higher self is the ferryman of one's destiny; to flow with the tide of life instead of throwing up mental dams, which block the connection between the personality and the source.

Gorse is also the Remedy for those who have been ill for a long time. It engenders hope, and hope is the first step towards recovery.

Positive potential following treatment: To know that all difficulties will be overcome in time.

ABOVE THE GORSE TYPE CAN HELP TO ALLEVIATE THEIR NEGATIVITY BY READING INSPIRATIONAL STORIES ABOUT PEOPLE WHO HAVE TRIUMPHED OVER ADVERSITY.

Other self-help measures: Read an uplifting novel or biography of one who has overcome difficulties against all odds.

If your surroundings at home are dull, make every effort to improve the situation. For example, put fresh flowers or potted plants around the house. If possible, re-decorate at least one room in your home with positive and joyful colours such as shades of yellow and gold, peach, clear greens and pinks.

Vapourize your favourite essential oil.

Commune with nature as often as possible.

The Gorse child: The Gorse Remedy will help uplift the spirits of the child who may have become despondent as a result of a long drawn out illness.

HEATHER (*Calluna vulgaris*)

A well-known evergreen shrub, turning huge areas of moorland purple in late summer. Flowers July–September. Blooms are mauve, pink and, occasionally, white.

Method of potentization: Sun.

Key negative state: Self-centredness; fear of loneliness; a poor listener.

ABOVE HEATHER IS A COMMON PLANT THAT CAN BE FOUND GROWING IN ABUNDANCE ON HEATH, MOORLAND AND WASTE GROUND.

Heather loves to talk – incessantly. She craves an audience and, indeed, has the uncanny knack of steering any conversation towards herself. No one else can get a word in edgeways!

Why should Heather be so self-centred? It has been said that she is the 'needy child', the lonely adult whose craving for affection and appreciation stems from a childhood starved of such necessities; thus she is unable to take any real interest in the needs of others.

53

The negative Heather state of mind can, of course, be temporary: when we are ill, for example, or going through a crisis such as bereavement, divorce or some other loss.

Positive potential following treatment: The gift of great empathy as a result of having suffered. To become a good listener. To be secure in oneself.

Other self-help measures: Make every effort to listen to others. Ask questions and wait for their reply.

Practise the aura strengthening visualization exercise (*see* p.105). By strengthening your own energy

ABOVE THE HEATHER TYPE IS SELF-CENTRED AND DEMANDS TO BE THE CENTRE OF ATTENTION. HE OR SHE TALKS RATHER THAN LISTENS.

field, the need to drain the energies of friends and family will be greatly diminished.

The Heather child: She will talk about herself with great exuberance, exaggerating along the way! In fact, the Heather state of mind is a natural childhood phase and should never be deemed a problem.

HOLLY (*Ilex aquifolium*)

A small evergreen tree or shrub with glossy, prickly, dark green leaves and red berries. Widespread in woods, hedgerows and thickets. The flowers are small and white, often tinged with purple. Blooms from May–August.

Method of potentization: Boiling.

Key negative state: Envy, jealousy, rage, suspicion or hatred.

Comparison: Compare with Willow who is an introvert and a depressive character who sees herself as a victim. Holly is a more active or intense type who can express his feelings with those whom he knows well.

ABOVE THE HOLLY BUSH HAS DARK SPIKY GREEN LEAVES. RED BERRIES APPEAR ON THE FEMALE PLANT IN THE AUTUMN.

The negative Holly state is the sub-personality residing within the psyche of each and every one of us. He is King of the Shadow, of envy, jealousy and spite. By nurturing the roots of hatred, he is the cause of every human difficulty, for hatred is the antithesis of the greatest force of all, that of love.

At times he may lurk ben-eath the surface, tending the smouldering coals of anger, contempt and resentment. If the flames of wrath are kept dampened for too long, however,

ABOVE PROFESSIONAL COUNSELLING MAY HELP THE JEALOUS AND ENVIOUS HOLLY TYPE LEARN HOW TO LOVE OTHERS.

54

and having no other outlet, they will invade our sleep in the guise of turbulent dreams, until we have no choice but to react with openly expressed venom!

Positive potential following treatment: The ability to give without thought of recompense; to rejoice in the good fortune of others, even when having problems oneself.

Other self-help measures: Instead of venting your wrath on family and friends, find an isolated spot. Then take a deep breath and scream or shout with all your might, releasing the pent up jealousy, anger, hatred – or whatever it might be. If isolation is impossible, scream or shout into a deep pillow or cushion to muffle the sound, then beat the hell out of it with your fists or a cricket bat!

Unfortunately, people who most need to let loose in this manner are often too reserved to do so – rationalizing their fear by calling the exercise childish, undignified or simply useless. A few may consider the exercise harmful, perhaps leading to a loss of self-control, or of one's sanity. Should this be so, then Cherry Plum may be indicated. Seek counselling or psychotherapy if you feel the need.

The Holly child: Holly is a most helpful Remedy during childhood, particularly when the first child is jealous of the new baby, for example.

HONEYSUCKLE (*Lonicera caprifolium*)

A beautifully fragrant woody climber, found in woodlands, on the edge of forests and in bushy places. The flowers of the variety used for the Remedy are reddish on the outside (not yellow as is most common), the inner surface white, but turning yellow on pollination. The flowers appear June–August.

Method of potentization: Boiling.

Key negative state: Nostalgia, regret, loss, homesickness.

Comparisons: Compare with Clematis whose thoughts are far away in the future, in happier times to come. Walnut, unlike Honeysuckle, feels the need to break with the past, but is finding the transition difficult.

BELOW HONEYSUCKLE, WHICH HAS A VERY STRONG SCENT, CAN BE FOUND GROWING IN WOODLAND AREAS.

Honeysuckle gazes out of the window dreaming of times gone by – of joy and laughter, tears and hardship, of missed opportunities and regrets. As she drifts further and further into the past, her life energies begin to stagnate in the inky pool of reminiscence, and thus she experiences a great loss of vitality. There is the danger that she may lose all interest in the issues and demands of the present. By the same token, she pays no heed to the life that lies ahead.

The Honeysuckle Remedy is of great comfort to the bereaved, or to the elderly person living alone. Others needing Honeysuckle are those who may have moved home or changed their job and now regret the action, dwelling on how much they miss their old life. Interestingly, the Remedy can also help those who cannot bear the thought of growing old and of losing their looks.

Positive potential following treatment: The ability to retain the lessons taught by past experiences, but not to cling to one's memories at the expense of the present.

Other self-help measures: Make every effort to occupy yourself with the present: for example, take an interest in current affairs programmes on radio and television. Take up activities that are 'grounding' such as gardening, dancing, cooking, pottery, keep-fit or some other form of physical exercise.

Try always to plan ahead, looking forward to events such as a holiday or an outing!

Mix with children – listen as well as talk to them.

The Honeysuckle child: She may suffer homesickness whilst staying with relatives; or she may have disturbing dreams caused by a recurrent upsetting memory.

HORNBEAM (*Carpinus betulus*)

A tree similar to the Beech, though smaller, reaching up to 19m. Found in woods and coppices. The pendant male and upright female flowers are green-brown, opening in April or May.

Method of potentization: Boiling.

Key negative state: Tiredness, weariness; that 'Monday morning' feeling.

Comparison: Compare with Olive whose exhaustion is more complete, born of physical and emotional strain as a result of a long illness or convalescence. With Hornbeam, it is always the thought of what lies ahead that causes the tiredness. 'Oh no, it's Monday,' groans Hornbeam, 'I feel even more tired this morning than I did before I went to bed last night.' Yet as soon as he begins work and becomes involved with his normal activities, the weariness disappears – until the next time!

In convalescence, Hornbeam is just the same, doubting that he has sufficient mental energy to return to work or simply to face the usual daily routine.

Positive potential following treatment: The ability and strength to cope with seemingly insurmountable difficulties. A renewed interest in life.

Other self-help measures: Make every effort to break your daily routine – take a different route to work; visit somewhere new at least

57

ABOVE HORNBEAM IS A STURDY DECIDUOUS TREE THAT IS COMMONLY USED FOR HEDGING. THE REMEDY IS USED TO GIVE STRENGTH AND CONFIDENCE.

once a week; read a different kind of book, magazine or newspaper from usual; take up a sport or new hobby and so on.

The Hornbeam child: This Remedy will be helpful for the child who is mentally sapped after the excitement (or strain) of returning to school after the holidays or after an illness.

IMPATIENS (*Impatiens glandulifera – I. roylei*)

A tall imposing balsam, growing to 180cm in height. Found by rivers and streams. Flowers vary from palest to fairly dark pinkish-mauve, though only the pale mauve flowers are used for the Remedy. Blooms from July–September.

Method of potentization: Sun.

Key negative state: Impatience and irritability.

She is quick in mind and body, suddenly flaring up when events do not move as swiftly as she would like. She blows hot and cold, pushing others to the point where they begin to feel like galley slaves. Yet, unlike Vine or Vervain, she is the unwilling leader, preferring to work alone and at her own pace.

In her more relaxed moments she will listen to advice, for Impatiens is essentially wise and open to new ideas. However, great restlessness is her guiding impulse. She sees things in a flash, making major decisions before anyone else can draw breath. But she often takes on too much, thus depleting her own energies and becoming bad-tempered and irritable.

ABOVE A NEW CHALLENGE SUCH AS TAKING UP A SPORT MAY HELP TO SHIFT THAT 'MONDAY MORNING' FEELING EXPERIENCED BY THE HORNBEAM TYPE.

Impatiens is included in the Rescue Remedy (*see* p.85) for its calming effect when trauma has caused a great deal of agitation.

Positive potential following treatment: Great empathy, patience and tolerance, especially towards the shortcomings of others.

Other self-help measures: Practise relaxation and deep breathing exercises (*see* pp.101–104); commune with nature as often as possible. Treat yourself to an aromatherapy massage once in a while.

For long-term benefits, take up yoga or Tai Chi, or try practising the Alexander Technique.

The Impatiens child: She is always irritable, constantly squabbling with other children or prone to temper tantrums. (However, if there is self-injury, turn to the Cherry Plum Remedy).

ABOVE THE ALEXANDER TECHNIQUE IS A GOOD SUPPORTIVE MEASURE FOR IMPATIENS TYPES.

59

LARCH (*Larix decidua*)

A tall graceful tree reaching up to 42m. Often found growing on the edge of hilly woodland. The male and female flowers appear on the same tree, golden yellow and bright red, respectively. The catkins (flowers) open in late March to early May.

Method of potentization: Boiling.

Key negative state: Lack of confidence.

Larch believes whole-heartedly that he is inferior to everyone else. Self-limitation has become deeply ingrained, reinforced by past

ABOVE LARCH IS THE ONLY CONIFER TO LOSE ITS LEAVES IN THE AUTUMN. THE REMEDY IS USED TO GIVE SELF-CONFIDENCE AND SELF-ESTEEM.

failures. Always he stands in the shadows allowing others (who are often less talented) to take his place in the limelight.

Dr Edward Bach described the Larch Remedy as the Flower that helps us become a little bolder so that we may plunge into life, seeking to our utmost; and in so doing, we may fulfil our purpose on Earth, which is to gain experience and knowledge.

Positive potential following treatment: Ceases to know the meaning of the word 'can't'. Becomes capable and determined; perseveres even when there are setbacks.

ABOVE LARCH IS FOR THOSE WHO HAVE POOR SELF-ESTEEM AND SUFFER FROM FEELINGS OF INFERIORITY. THE REMEDY WILL ENCOURAGE BOLDNESS.

Other self-help measures: Dreamwork; (*see* pp.26–27); Seek counselling if necessary.

Develop new skills by enrolling on an adult education course. If you can afford to work without pay, do some voluntary work. The experience will be enriching, not only enhancing future job prospects, but more importantly, boosting your self-esteem.

The Larch child: Like the adult, he feels unable to venture on his own, has low self-esteem and needs a great deal of gentle encouragement from his parents and teachers.

MIMULUS (*Mimulus guttatus*)

An attractive creeping plant, about 30cm in height, found growing in wet places, especially near shallow streams. The bright yellow flowers open June to September.

Method of potentization: Sun.

Key negative state: Fear of known things such as flying, certain animals, public speaking, going to the dentist.

Comparison: Compare with Rock Rose whose fear is extremely acute – it may be the result of a terrifying accident, for example. The Mimulus fear is less acute and is of a general nature. However, if actually experiencing panic as a result of an encounter with the object of your fear (for example, a spider), then take Rock Rose or Rescue Remedy. Regular doses of Mimulus will help to lessen, and eventually transmute, the fear.

Sensitive, retiring Mimulus sits in the corner, both hands clutching a glass of sherry. She would rather not be here but forceful Vervain has persuaded her to join the 'fun' of the office party. She finds the laughing, shrieking exuberance of the other members of staff intimidating. She looks longingly at the fire-escape door, planning her exit.

Positive potential following treatment: Quiet courage to face trials and difficulties; becoming understanding and supportive of others in a similar situation.

Other self-help measures: Dream-work (*see* pp.26–27); practise the aura strengthening visualization (*see* p.105).

If you suffer from a specific phobia such as cats, open spaces and so forth, you may also need to seek professional counselling. In addition, accept that sensitivity is a fine gift, and can be put to positive use such as counselling others or performing healing work of any nature.

RIGHT MIMULUS GROWS IN BOGGY SITES. ITS YELLOW FLOWERS APPEAR IN MIDSUMMER.

Repeat the following affirmation before you go to sleep at night: 'I connect with my higher self, which is love. Where there is love, there is no fear.'

The Mimulus child: She may fear the dark, other children, animals or even the swimming pool.

MUSTARD (*Sinapis arvensis*)

A very common annual 30–60cm in height, growing in fields and by the wayside. The brilliant yellow flowers appear from May to July.

Method of potentization: Boiling.

Key negative state: Fluctuating cycles of black depression.

Mustard has everything anyone could ever wish for on the Earthly plane – a lovely wife, two beautiful children, no financial worries, and a wonderful home – but for many years he has been victim to fluctuating cycles of melancholia. Without warning, and for no apparent reason, a heavy black cloud descends upon him, stifling the sunshine and joy out of life. The mood may remain for days or weeks, until it eventually lifts as suddenly as it came, only to return again later in all its engulfing darkness.

Positive potential following treatment: Inner serenity; the ability to transmute melancholia into joy and peace.

Other self-help measures: It may at first seem like masochism, but by acknowledging and accepting the Mustard state for what it is – a chance for one's spirit to learn and grow – we may pass through the gloom towards the light of the higher self. By fighting the negativity, which is just like tensing up against physical pain, we only succeed in giving it more energy. So, instead, enter fully into the mood – read a sad novel, listen to melancholic music, indulge in nostalgia – the Flower Remedy will see you through. Take up Tai Chi, which also teaches the art of yielding to force in order to weaken it.

Counselling or psychotherapy will help if you feel you really cannot work through the depression alone.

The Mustard child: If a child is showing the symptoms described above do seek expert help as well as giving the Remedy. If your doctor can only prescribe drugs, consider consulting a holistic therapist or a reputable spiritual healer (see Useful Addresses, pp.124–125).

OAK (*Quercus robur*)

The majestic English Oak can reach a height of 30m and is extremely long-lived, possibly up to 800 years. In the past much of Britain was covered in Oak forests. The male and female flowers develop on the same tree, opening at the end of April to early May.

Method of potentization: Sun.

Key negative state: Despondency as a result of obstinate, relentless effort against all odds.

Hard-working Oak has reserves of energy and willpower that are truly amazing. She leaves other resourceful people such as Vervain and Vine in the shade. When despondency does eventually set in, as a result of unceasing effort, she refuses to give in to ill-health or adversity. Rarely does she seek advice or help, hiding her tiredness from others lest they should discover her 'weakness'. As a consequence, of course, her life is always an uphill struggle.

Unfortunately, such an attitude could lead to a nervous breakdown. Life's lesson for Oak is to realize

ABOVE OAK LEAVES AND FLOWERS APPEAR IN LATE SPRING. MALE AND FEMALE FLOWERS BOTH GROW ON THE SAME TREE.

63

ABOVE THE OAK REMEDY IS FOR THOSE WHO WORK TOO HARD, EXHAUSTING THEMSELVES IN THE PROCESS.

that hard work and achievement has its place, but is not the sole purpose of our existence. We also need frivolity and those precious moments of gentle tears – like the soft summer rain that refreshes and revitalizes the parched meadows.

Positive potential following treatment: The ability to overcome all life's problems with courage; to become strong, patient and full of common sense.

Other self-help measures: Seek some frivolity in life! Take up yoga to encourage flexibility of mind and body.

The Oak child: Like the adult, she works very hard, viewing her schoolwork as some vital duty that must be done well at all costs. Unlike Elm who may momentarily lose confidence, Oak carries on, pushing herself to the limits of endurance even though it may have become useless. Consider deeply whether the child is being pushed by over-ambitious parents.

64

OLIVE (*Olea europaea*)

A small evergreen tree native to the Mediterranean. Only wild trees are used for the Remedy. The small whitish clusters of flowers appear on the numerous thin branches in the spring, usually April or May.

Method of potentization: Sun.

Key negative state: Complete mental and physical exhaustion.

ABOVE NATIVE TO THE
MEDITERRANEAN, THE OLIVE TREE HAS
SILVERY GREEN LEAVES AND BEARS
EDIBLE FRUITS.

Comparison: Compare with Hornbeam whose weariness is more of the mind, that 'Monday morning' feeling`. The Olive exhaustion is complete, of both mind and body, the result of over-exertion during childbirth, for example, or after a long illness. Indeed, so great is his weariness even the things that once gave him joy are no longer pleasurable.

Positive potential following treatment: Peace of mind; vitality; a renewed interest in life.

Other self-help measures: If total exhaustion has become a way of life, and is not simply the result of a stint of hard work, do have a medical check-up and/or consult a well qualified holistic therapist such as a homeopath or medical herbalist.

ABOVE VISIT A PROFESSIONAL HOMEOPATH IF EXHAUSTION BECOMES A CONSTANT PROBLEM.

Look after yourself – get plenty of sleep, fresh air, sunshine and adequate exercise – a revitalizing combination. Eat sensibly; practise the deep breathing, relaxation and aura strengthening visualization exercises (*see* p.105).

The Olive child: The Remedy is invaluable to children during illness and convalescence, acting as a strengthener.

PINE (*Pinus sylvestris*)

The only Pine indigenous to Britain, found growing wild in Scotland, but much planted elsewhere. Grows to a height of 36m, its bark is browny-red lower down, orangey-brown and flaky in the upper crown. Male and female flowers appear on the same tree; yellow and red respectively. Flowers May–June.

Method of potentization: Boiling.

Key negative state: Self-reproach; guilt.

The Pine type carries the burden of original sin in her heart – not only blaming herself for the mistakes of others, but also apologizing for her very existence, believing that self-punishment is her only true chance of redemption. 'Ouch! I'm so sorry,' she says, when someone steps on her toes.

Unlike Larch, who will not try for fear of failure, Pine will often forge ahead, only to become depressed when she fails to live up to her own high ideals – which incidentally she would never impose upon other people.

Her life's lesson is to realize that regret is fine, but we must also forgive ourselves and learn from our mistakes.

Positive potential following treatment: The ability to feel regret rather than guilt; self-forgiveness; to take responsibility with a fair and balanced attitude.

Other self-help measures: In a meditative state, or whilst lying down deeply relaxed (*see* pp.101–102), ask that you may be given an animal (an imaginary creature) to love and nurture. Whatever animal comes to mind, accept this as representing your higher self. Feed the creature, stroke its soft fur, smooth feathers or warm shiny back – radiate feelings of warmth and love. See that the creature responds joyfully to your touch. How could you ever punish such a beautiful being? Know that retribution is unnecessary, for your past mistakes are already forgiven. Practise this visualization at least twice a week for as long as you feel the need. At other times, whenever guilty feelings rise to the fore, think of your creature.

The Pine child: This child tends to be the scapegoat in class, taking the blame for the mistakes of others, and accepting the punishment without complaint.

RIGHT PINE IS FOR THOSE WHO CARRY A BURDEN OF GUILT AND SELF-BLAME. THIS REMEDY WILL HELP TO REGAIN A BLANCED SENSE OF RESPONSIBILITY.

RED CHESTNUT (*Aesculus carnea*)

This tree is less robust than the Common or White Chestnut, reaching up to 18–25m. The strong rose-pink flowers appear in pyramidal clusters in late May or early June.

Method of potentization: Boiling.

Key negative state: Fear and excessive concern for the welfare of others.

ABOVE THE LEAVES AND FLOWERS OF THE CHESTNUT TREE, WHICH IS OFTEN TO BE FOUND IN PARKS.

It is perfectly natural to be apprehensive for our loved ones when they embark on some new or risky venture, or when they are ill, but the Red Chestnut type's fear is out of all proportion to the event. Indeed, Red Chestnut habitually worries about the welfare of his loved ones, smothering them with his concern.

67

Red Chestnut is also the Remedy for those who feel distressed as a result of reading or hearing about some terrible disaster in another part of the world. Such individuals identify strongly with suffering and experience a sense of overwhelming powerlessness. As Bach said, our negative thoughts harm not only ourselves, but also those to whom they are projected.

Positive potential following treatment: The ability to send out thoughts of safety, health or courage to those who need

LEFT THE RED CHESTNUT PARENT IS OVERPROTECTIVE AND FEARS THAT SOME AWFUL HARM WILL BEFALL THEIR CHILD. THE REMEDY WILL HELP TO RATIONALIZE THIS ANXIETY.

them; to keep a cool head in emergencies; to remain calm both physically and mentally.

Other self-help measures: Practise the aura strengthening visualization (*see* p.105). Train yourself to imagine the person for whom you feel concern safely enclosed within their own sphere of light. Try not always to imagine the worst – a plane crash, car accident, or whatever – instead, see the person in your mind's eye arriving home safely and smiling!

The Red Chestnut child: He may have been given a great deal of responsibility at an early age, perhaps caring for a new baby, or he could be reflecting the attitude of a parent.

ROCK ROSE (*Helianthemum nummularium*)

A low, spreading, shrubby plant found on chalk downs, limestone and gravelly soils. The bright yellow flowers open, usually two at a time, from June–September.

Method of potentization: Sun.

Key negative state: Extremely acute state of fear, terror or panic; helplessness.

Comparisons: Compare with Aspen whose fear is of the mind that something dreadful is about to happen, but not knowing what it may be. The Mimulus fear is of known things – fear of loneliness or of animals, for example. The Rock Rose fear is sheer terror, so serious as to cause intense fear in those around.

ABOVE THE ROCK ROSE SPECIES HAS BRIGHT YELLOW FLOWERS. THEY ARE SHORT-LIVED AND WILL SOON FALL WHEN PICKED.

The negative Rock Rose state of mind only occurs temporarily during a crisis, for example, when there is great terror at the site of a horrific accident. For this reason, Rock Rose is included in the Rescue Remedy (*see* p.85). Rock Rose is also helpful to those who suffer from panic attacks triggered by stress.

Positive potential following treatment: Great courage – a willingness to risk one's own life for others.

ABOVE ROCK ROSE IS ONE OF THE INGREDIENTS IN BACH'S RESCUE REMEDY, THE REMEDY FOR ALL KINDS OF EMERGENCIES.

Other self-help measures: This is not usually possible in an emergency.

If you suffer from panic attacks, practise deep breathing, relaxation, meditation and nature attunement (*see* chapter 7) and Dreamwork (*see* pp.26–27).

Counselling or psychotherapy may also be necessary.

The Rock Rose child: This Remedy helps the child who may wake screaming from a nightmare.

ROCK WATER

This is not a plant but potentized spring water, formerly prepared by Bach from the spring at Sotwell near Mount Vernon. As this source is no longer available, the Bach Centre uses a spring in Wales that Bach used before he came to Mount Vernon. Incidentally, any spring that is still left free and in its natural state (not the wells and springs over which

ABOVE THE ROCK WATER REMEDY IS PREPARED FROM PURE SPRING WATER THAT HAS BEEN FILTERED BY ROCK.

69

chapels and shrines have been built) can be used for the Remedy.

Method of potentization: Sun.

Key negative state: A too rigid self discipline leading to repression and self-denial.

Though Rock Water would never openly criticize others, she tries to set a good example at all times, and is proud of her stringent and disciplined lifestyle. Yet if the truth be known, her spirit yearns for the freedom of spontaneity, laughter and tears – for the sheer joy of living life to the full.

Of course, the Rock Water type is also recognized in the fanatical keep-fit enthusiast, or in the person who is always on a stringent diet. In fact, most of us need the Remedy from time to time, when our needs are consciously or unconsciously denied.

Positive potential following treatment: An open minded idealism; sufficient conviction not to be easily influenced by others. To radiate joy and peace, thus being a natural example to others.

Other self-help measures: Seek some frivolity in life! Allow yourself a few luxuries – a cream cake, a lie-in on a Sunday morning, a lazy holiday and so on.

The Rock Water child: Not a state normally associated with childhood, though the Remedy may help the pernickety eater.

SCLERANTHUS (*Scleranthus annuus*)

A small, easily overlooked, wiry, rather bushy annual, 50–70cm high. Grows in cornfields on sandy and gravelly soils. The pale or darker green clusters of minute, petalless flowers appear July to September.

Method of potentization: Sun.

Key negative state: Indecision, uncertainty, mood swings.

Erratic Scleranthus never quite knows whether he is coming or going, always being swayed between two possibilities –'Should I wear the blue shirt or the green?' he asks himself (for unlike Cerato he rarely seeks advice). Even when he does make up his mind, he is certain to change it again. Thus, it is hardly surprising that others regard him as somewhat unreliable, or a time-waster.

In illness, true to form, Scleranthus cannot decide where in his body he feels discomfort, the symptoms tending to move about, first here then there, irritating his doctor beyond measure!

LEFT SCLERANTHUS HAS MINUTE GREEN FLOWERS. THE REMEDY IS FOR INDECISIVENESS AND AN INABILITY TO CHOOSE BETWEEN ALTERNATIVES.

It is interesting to note that the Scleranthus Remedy can also be of help in motion or travel sickness.

Positive potential following treatment: The ability to make a decision quickly and to act promptly; to maintain poise and balance whatever the circumstances.

Other self-help measures: As for Cerato (*see* pp.40–41).

The Scleranthus child: Like the adult, the Scleranthus child is subject to extremes of mood, crying one minute, smiling the next.

During illness, symptoms move about or swing from one polarity to the other: constipation then diarrhoea, hot then cold, ravenous hunger then loss of appetite, and so on.

ABOVE THE SCLERANTHUS CHILD IS SUBJECT TO WILD MOOD SWINGS, HAPPILY SMILING AND CHATTING AWAY ONE MINUTE, CRYING PITIFULLY THE NEXT.

STAR OF BETHLEHEM

(*Ornithogalum umbellatum*)

A slender-leaved plant related to the onion and garlic. It grows to a height of 15–30cm and is found in woods and meadows. The flowers are striped green on the outside and brilliant white inside, opening only in bright sunlight. Flowers from April–June.

Method of potentization: Boiling.

ABOVE STAR OF BETHLEHEM HAS DELICATE SIX-POINTED STAR-SHAPED PURE WHITE FLOWERS. THE REMEDY IS USED FOR SHOCK AND TRAUMA.

Key negative state: Shock, both physical and mental.

Star of Bethlehem, the Remedy for shock, is regarded by many Bach Flower practitioners as the most important component of the Rescue Remedy (*see* p.85), harmonizing with the other four Flowers that make up the Remedy, yet also triggering the action of the whole.

Although not a Type Remedy, Star of Bethlehem can help those who suffer from long-term physical or emotional distress as a result of past trauma, for example the shock of an accident, bereavement or divorce.

The effect of shock can also be so delayed that many years might pass before the full impact is felt.

This delayed or repressed shock may manifest as feelings of guilt, depression, anxiety, anger – or perhaps in the guise of some physical complaint.

Although it is best to treat shock as soon as possible, Star of Bethlehem can often be the catalyst required if shock has been sustained and can be identified as the cause of a person's problems.

Positive potential following treatment: A neutralization of the effects of shock and trauma, whether they were immediate or delayed.

Other self-help measures: Though not usually possible in an emergency, the following therapies may be helpful for any delayed or unrealized reactions – aromatherapy massage (neroli essential oil is often indicated); spiritual healing (*see* Useful Addresses, pp.124–125).

The Star of Bethlehem child: Star of Bethlehem Remedy can be given to newborn babies (perhaps in the baby's bath water) to help neutralize the shock of being born into the world.

SWEET CHESTNUT (*Castanea sativa*)

The tree can reach up to 30m in open woodlands and parks. As it matures, the thick, grey-brown, deeply furrowed bark begins to twist into beautiful spirals around the trunk.

ABOVE THE LEAVES AND FRUITS OF THE SWEET CHESTNUT TREE.

The sickly scented, pale yellow catkin-like flowers appear after the leaves, from June–August.

Method of potentization: Boiling.

Key negative state: Extreme mental anguish; the utmost limits of endurance; unable even to pray.

Comparisons: Compare with Mustard whose depression comes and goes like a black cloud, the cause unknown. The Sweet Chestnut depression is triggered by some life-shattering event, yet unlike the Cherry Plum state, does not lead to suicidal feelings. Like Agrimony, Sweet Chestnut tries to hide her distress from others.

Sweet Chestnut sits slumped against the wall, desperately and utterly alone, her life shattered into a million pieces. There is no more yesterday or tomorrow, merely a dark foreboding present. Even death itself offers no true release, for the pain touches her very soul.

That is the extent of the negative Sweet Chestnut state of mind. The Remedy helps to unfreeze time, allowing the sun to rise again. And as it becomes brighter, an image of hope and new life appears on the horizon – the Phoenix emerging from the ashes.

73

BELOW SPIRITUAL HEALING MAY BENEFIT THOSE SWEET CHESTNUT TYPES WHOSE ANGUISH AND DESPAIR ARE UNBEARABLE.

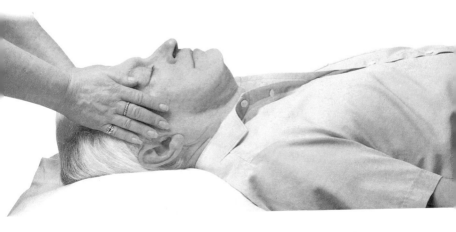

Positive potential following treatment: Hope returns; the end of torment is at last within reach. She has personal experiences of the true meaning of life, and/or of the Godhead.

Other self-help measures: Not usually possible in the acute stage, especially if one is trapped in a war zone, for instance, or caught up in some other catastrophe. However, during the recovery period, try to commune with nature as often as possible, and consider having some spiritual healing (*see* Useful Addresses, pp.124–125).

The Sweet Chestnut child: The Remedy may be indicated for the child suffering mental anguish as a result of parental divorce or bereavement.

74

VERVAIN (*Verbena officinalis*)

A rough hairy perennial, 30–60cm high. Widespread on dry, grassy ground, especially on chalk and limestone. The spikes of small lilac-coloured flowers open from June to September.

Method of potentization: Sun.

Key negative state: Strain and tension as a result of over-enthusiasm; hyperanxiety.

Comparison: Compare with Vine who is pushy and domineering in order to achieve her own egotistical ends. Vervain is motivated by concern for the welfare of others; a desire to enthuse and convert.

Vervain is prone to over-enthusiasm, some might say fanaticism. He lives on his nerves and is quite unable to relax. As a consequence, he suffers from stiffness and muscle pain, and sometimes headaches or pain in the eyes. His guiding impulse is the urge to convert others to his way of thinking. Although it could be said that his heart is

ABOVE VERVAIN IS A ROADSIDE PLANT THAT HAS LONG SPIKES OF PINKISH FLOWERS. THE REMEDY IS FOR STRONG-MINDED PEOPLE WHO THINK THEY ARE ALWAYS RIGHT.

in the right place, he is apt to put others off by bombarding them with his arguments. Rarely does he listen to any other point of view. Incensed by injustice, he takes the side of the underdog, initiating pressure groups and standing on committees.

His life's lesson is to realize that too much pressure only produces counterpressure and squanders one's own energies in the process. As Dr Bach said, it is often by being rather than doing that great things are accomplished.

Positive potential following treatment: The ability to step back from time to time and to relax when necessary. The realization that others have a right to their opinions. The wisdom to change one's mind as a result of discussion and good argument.

Other self-help measures: Although deep breathing and relaxation exercises are needed, it may be easier to begin by taking up some form of physical activity that counteracts rigidity of body and mind, such as Tai Chi, yoga or a martial art. Also, try to commune with nature as often as possible.

Have some massage therapy or aromatherapy or learn the Alexander Technique.

The Vervain child: This child is tense and frustrated, perhaps also hyperactive; has difficulty sleeping, or needs less sleep than average.

VINE (*Vitis vinifera*)
A long-lived climber, growing to a length of 15m or more. Indigenous to warmer countries such as Greece and the south of France. The flowers are small, green and fragrant, appearing in the spring. Only the wild Vine is used for the Flower Remedy.

Method of potentization: Sun.

Key negative state: A domineering, bullying and inflexible personality, who is always striving for power and is ruthlessly ambitious.

ABOVE ALTHOUGH WIDELY CULTIVATED FOR ITS FRUIT, ONLY THE WILD VINE IS USED FOR THE FLOWER REMEDY.

Comparison: Compare with Vervain who tries to convince others through explanation and debate. Vine will not argue the matter, stating her point of view and expecting others to obey her command.

Vine rules her household like a warrior queen; the children – and even the dog – literally standing to attention whenever she barks her orders. At work, she is no different, terrorizing all those who dare to cross her path. Interestingly, as Bach Flower practitioner Mechthild Scheffer points out, the negative Vine state sometimes appears together with weaker characteristics such as those of Mimulus, Pine or Larch. The weaknesses within the personality are over-compensated for by excessive will-power and hardness.

ABOVE VINE IS BOSSY AND DOMINATING, WITH A TENDENCY TO BULLY ALL AROUND HER. THE VINE REMEDY WILL HELP THE VINE TYPE TO RESPECT OTHERS.

Positive potential following treatment: To become the wise and compassionate ruler, leader or teacher who inspires others; to use one's great qualities of leadership to guide rather than to dominate.

Other self-help measures: For Vine even to recognize that she needs help is a great step forward indeed. She may only have reached such a state of awareness after being given the Remedy surreptitiously (in her tea perhaps) by her long-suffering husband!

76

Take up yoga or Tai Chi; try Dreamwork (*see* pp.26–27); and, if necessary, consider counselling or psychotherapy, particularly group work, which encourages a sense of unity.

The Vine child: This child is always the leader of the gang, or the school captain; she tends to be aggressive, and in the extreme can become a bully.

WALNUT (*Juglans regia*)

A beautiful tree growing to about 30m. Grows well in orchards and other protected places. The male catkins and small green female flowers appear on the same tree. Blooms in April and May, before or just after the leaf-buds burst.

Method of potentization: Boiling.

Key negative state: Difficulties adjusting to change of any nature. Oversensitivity to ideas and influences.

Comparison: Unlike Honeysuckle, Walnut desires to move on, but finds it difficult to break the link with the past or with certain relationships.

ABOVE THE WALNUT TREE BEARS EDIBLE NUTS. THE REMEDY IS USEFUL DURING TIMES OF TRANSITION SUCH AS MARRIAGE, LEAVING HOME OR CHANGING CAREERS.

The negative Walnut state is usually of a passing nature. It is the Remedy for those who have difficulty adjusting to a new situation, be it a change of job, a new home, marriage, divorce, parenthood or whatever.

The Remedy helps to break the link with the past so that life can start afresh. Walnut also proves useful in any physical change such as teething, puberty, pregnancy and the menopause. Many women have found the Remedy helpful during the pre-menstrual phase. It is usually combined with Scleranthus (for mood swings) and with other Flowers accordingly.

Walnut is also used by Bach Flower practitioners and Healers alike as a means of 'psychic protection' (*see* p.104).

77

Positive potential following treatment: Having the determination to carry through one's ideals and ambitions, despite adverse circumstances, damning comments and ridicule.

Other self-help measures: Read *Cutting the Ties that Bind* by Phyllis Krystal; and repeat the following affirmation before you go to sleep at night: 'I follow the guidance of my higher self.'

The Walnut child: As well as helping during the various milestones of a child's development (for instance, teething, starting school and puberty). Walnut can also help with adjustment to other changes; for example, staying away from home for

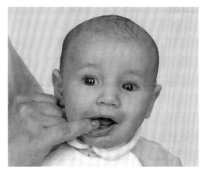

ABOVE AS THE REMEDY FOR TEMPORARY CHANGE, WALNUT CAN HELP WITH TRANSITIONS THAT OCCUR DURING CHILDHOOD DEVELOPMENT, SUCH AS TEETHING.

the first time or when the child is suffering as the result of parental divorce, changing home or school.

WATER VIOLET (*Hottonia palustris*)

A graceful, floating, almost hairless perennial plant found growing in ditches and ponds, the finely divided leaves remaining under the surface of the water. Spikes of pale lilac-white flowers appear in May and June.

Method of potentization: Sun.

Key negative state: Pride and aloofness.

Water Violet stands alone, serene and self-contained. She is the wise teacher, the therapist, the peacemaker, the one who is sought after for advice. Yet her role is that of the listening counsellor rather than the assertive adviser, for she never attempts to interfere or influence, and similarly will not share her own problems or health concerns with others. Therefore, when unwell Water Violet prefers to be left alone. Likewise, she has been known to bear even the deepest grief with silent dignity.

Water Violet runs the risk of becoming too self-contained and aloof; that same veil of superior separateness hardening into an impenetrable armour, thus isolating her from the rest of humanity. Others then tend to regard her as cold, conceited or supercilious. As a consequence, she experiences the true meaning of loneliness within her self-built ivory tower of pride.

Positive potential following treatment: Although remaining comfortable with one's own company, one will have the wisdom and sympathy to put one's capabilities to the service of other people.

Other self-help measures: Activities or hobbies that are 'grounding' – for example, gardening, sport, pottery, cooking, dancing, walking, giving and/or receiving massage.

ABOVE SUPPORTIVE MEASURES FOR THE WATER VIOLET TYPE INCLUDE GROUNDING ACTIVITIES SUCH AS WALKING.

79

The Water Violet child: Like the adult, rather proud and independent, an unusual child. She can spend many hours alone, playing contentedly.

WHITE CHESTNUT (*Aesculus hippocastanum*)

The common Horse Chestnut tree can reach up to about 30m. The flowers are white with a patch of yellow-turning-to-red on the petal bases. The 'candelabra' clusters appear at the end of May to early June.

Method of potentization: Sun.

Key negative state: Persistent worrying thoughts and mental arguments.

Comparison: Unlike Clematis the daydreamer who is happy to escape from the world, White Chestnut would give anything to escape from his thoughts into the world.

ABOVE THE FRUIT AND LEAVES OF THE COMMON HORSE CHESTNUT TREE. THE REMEDY IS USED TO BRING PEACE OF MIND AND MENTAL CLARITY.

White Chestnut suffers from a carousel mind, the same old arguments spinning round and round in his head, never reaching a satisfactory conclusion, interrupting his sleep and causing a great deal of distress. He feels exhausted and is unable to concentrate. As a consequence, he can be somewhat accident-prone and tends not to hear when he is spoken to.

Positive potential following treatment: Peace of mind and a solution to one's problems.

Other self-help measures: Occasionally, an overactive mind leading to insomnia can be indicative of a deficiency of zinc coupled with an excess of copper and/or other nutritional deficiencies. For more information read *The Wright Diet* by Celia Wright.

Commune with nature as often as possible, and combine this with a physical activity such as brisk walking, hill or mountain walking, swimming, cycling. Yoga is also beneficial for the White Chestnut type.

ABOVE TAKE ZINC SUPPLEMENTS IF YOU THINK THAT YOU MAY BE SUFFERING FROM A DEFICIENCY OF THIS MINERAL.

80

The White Chestnut child: The Remedy has proved helpful to older children suffering from insomnia as a result of excessive study during the examination term.

WILD OAT (*Bromus ramosus*) A grass commonly found as a weed on arable land, in damp woods and thickets and by roadsides. The flowers appear in July and August.

ABOVE WILD OAT BELONGS TO THE GRASS FAMILY. IT CAN COMMONLY BE FOUND GROWING IN HEDGES AND WOODS.

Method of potentization: Sun.

Key negative state: Dissatisfaction because one's true vocation has not been found. Boredom and frustration.

Comparison: Make a comparison with Scleranthus who vacillates between two possibilities, even the most trivial. Wild Oat is uncertain about her life's mission, but is otherwise decisive and clear-headed.

81

Wild Oat is the rambling rover, a lost soul who has yet to find her true niche in life. She has travelled far and wide, lived one lifestyle then another and has had a variety of jobs, yet still she searches for that elusive state known as fulfilment. Her lesson is to realize the benefits of channelling her talents towards a single goal, for to scatter her energies in all directions serves only to sow the seeds of discontent.

LEFT MEDITATION WILL HELP THE WILD OAT TYPE TO FOCUS THE MIND AND DISCOVER JUST WHAT SHE WANTS TO DO WITH HER LIFE.

Positive potential following treatment: The realization of one's true vocation in life.

Other self-help measures: Meditation to help focus your attention in one direction (*see* pp.107–109).

Repeat the following affirmation before you go to sleep at night: 'I follow the guidance of my higher self.'

The Wild Oat child: This child is usually very able but, like the adult, tends to scatter her energies, rarely identifying with any particular peer group.

WILD ROSE (*Rosa canina*)

The 'English Rose' is widespread in sunny hedgerows and thickets, though rare in Scotland. The fragrant flowers are white, pale pink or deep pink, opening singly or in groups of three between June and August.

82

Method of potentization: Boiling.

Key negative state: Resignation and apathy.

The Wild Rose type exists without joy or pleasure, making little effort to get well, or to find employment that he enjoys. He accepts illness, misfortune and monotony without complaint as if they were a penance decreed by fate for the 'sins of the fathers' no doubt.

ABOVE WILD ROSE IS A VIGOROUS CLIMBING PLANT THAT GROWS IN HEDGEROWS. THE REMEDY IS GOOD FOR APATHY.

Positive potential following treatment: A renewed interest in life and, with the return of one's vitality, the enrichment and enjoyment of friendship and good health.

Other self-help measures: As well as taking the Flower Remedies, you may also need some other therapy to release the flow of vital energies, for example, acupuncture, spiritual healing, colour healing and psychotherapy. This is especially true if the Wild Rose state of mind has been a way of life for some considerable time.

The Wild Rose child: Seek expert advice from your health practitioner if this state of mind has become chronic.

It is common for a mild Wild Rose state to emerge during adolescence, though it is usually a passing phase.

WILLOW (*Salix vitellina*)

A small tree reaching up to 10m found growing on moist and low-lying ground. The flexible branches are used for basket-making. In winter, the twigs turn a bright orange-yellow. The male and female catkins grow on different trees, opening in April and May.

ABOVE ACUPUNCTURE WILL HELP TO UNBLOCK THE FLOW OF VITAL ENERGIES, GIVING THE WILD ROSE TYPE A NEW ZEST FOR LIFE.

Method of potentization: Boiling.

Key negative state: Bitterness, resentment, depression, self-pity.

Comparison: Compare with Holly who is not a depressive by nature and can more easily express anger and jealousy. Willow is much more withdrawn and depressed, seeing herself as a victim.

Sulky, grumbling Willow blames the rest of humanity or God for her 'miserable and cruel' lot in life. Never for a moment does she consider that her own attitude might be at fault. She has no interest whatsoever in others except to speak with bitterness and unkindness of their good fortune. Therefore, she considers it her 'right' to accept all kinds of help without a word of gratitude. Not surprisingly, she has succeeded in driving away many a friend or relative who initially offered her

LEFT THE LEAVES OF THE WILLOW TREE ARE SLENDER AND GRACEFUL. THE TREE CAN OFTEN BE FOUND GROWING NEAR WATER.

their help, understanding and friendship. Of course, she will hold a grudge against such deserters for all eternity. Thus, her distress turns inwards whereupon it eats away at her heart.

Many of us need a dose of Willow from time to time, especially on those days when nothing seems to go right and we begin to begrudge the happiness or good fortune of others.

Positive potential following treatment: Optimism and a sense of humour; the ability to accept responsibility for one's own life and health and to see things in their true perspective.

Other self-help measures: Begin to take more responsibility for your own life and health by finding out as much as you can about the philosophy and practice of holism.

If you can afford to work without payment, take up some voluntary work, or offer to help your friends, relatives or neighbours; for it is only by giving that we truly receive. Also, practise saying 'thank you', and progress to 'I love you'.

Commune with nature as often as possible; and see also the self-help exercise suggested for Holly.

The Willow child: She is sulky and resentful, but the reason for her distress is not always apparent. When lightly scolded for some misdemeanour, she feels she does not deserve so great a punishment.

RIGHT THE WILLOW CHILD IS SULKY AND SELFISH. SHE CAN OFTEN BE HEARD SAYING 'IT'S NOT FAIR'.

84

Rescue Remedy

This is composite of five of the 38 Flowers. As its name suggests, it is the Remedy for all emergencies – when there is panic, shock, hysteria, mental numbness, even unconsciousness. Although the Remedy cannot replace medical attention, it can alleviate much of the person's distress whilst they await the arrival of medical aid, thus enabling the body/mind's healing processes to commence without delay.

Rescue Remedy is also most helpful in other traumatic situations such as visiting the dentist, receiving bad news, after an argument or when a child is distressed after seeing horror or violence on television, and so on.

Bach advised that we should carry a small bottle of Rescue Remedy with us at all times. It is also a good idea to keep a bottle in the bathroom cabinet or in the first-aid box.

The five Flowers that make up the Rescue Remedy are:

Star of Bethlehem: for shock and numbness;

Rock Rose: for terror and panic;

Impatiens: for great agitation, irritability and tension;

Cherry Plum: for violent outbursts and hysteria;

Clematis: for the bemused, faraway sensation that often precedes a faint, and for unconsciousness.

85

DOSAGES AND OTHER APPLICATIONS

Flower Remedies are modestly priced and economical to use. For example, a 10ml bottle of Stock Concentrate, if diluted correctly, will provide approximately 60 treatments. Although the Stock Concentrates keep indefinitely, once diluted in water they will keep for no longer than three to four weeks.

PREPARATION OF THE TREATMENT

The standard dilution is 2 drops from each Stock Concentrate to a 30ml dropper medicine bottle, ¾ filled with spring water and topped up with brandy or cider vinegar (which act as preservatives).

DOSAGE

GENERAL USE
Take 4 drops of the diluted Remedy on the tongue three to four times daily. Alternatively, you can add the same number of drops to a small glass of spring water, fruit juice or any other beverage.

For acute conditions (*see* p.89–91), there is no need to prepare a treatment bottle, just add 2 drops of the Stock (4 of Rescue Remedy) directly into a glass or cup of spring water and sip at intervals. It is most beneficial to hold the dose in your mouth for a few seconds before swallowing, and to visualize the Flower vibrations flooding your whole being.

BABIES AND NURSING MOTHERS

The number of drops used for infant dosage (and for older children) is the same as for adults. Four drops of the diluted Remedy is added to the baby's bottle, or taken in a teaspoonful of boiled water or fruit juice, four times daily. Nursing mothers can take the Remedies themselves, diluted in spring water. The Flower vibrations will then be imparted to the baby through the mother's milk.

ABOVE TO TREAT ACUTE CONDITIONS, SIMPLY ADD 2 DROPS OF STOCK CONCENTRATE TO A GLASS OF SPRING WATER OR FRUIT JUICE.

87

ANIMALS

Rescue Remedy is the main basic Remedy for animal treatment. The normal dosage for domestic pets is 4 drops of Rescue (2 drops of any other Flower) in drinking water or milk. For larger animals such as horses, give 10 drops of Rescue (5 drops of any other Flower) to a bucket of water; or, if easier to administer, 4 drops of undiluted Rescue, 2 of any other chosen Flower, on a sugar lump.

ABOVE FOR DOGS AND OTHER SMALL DOMESTIC ANIMALS, ADD 2 DROPS OF RESCUE REMEDY TO THEIR DRINKING WATER.

PLANTS

The Bach Centre suggests 10 drops of each chosen Flower to a large watering can. A plant that has been accidentally uprooted needs Rescue Remedy for shock, and probably Walnut too if it has to be transplanted. As a general garden tonic, especially when plants have become weakened by pests, a combination of Rescue Remedy and Crab Apple is recommended. To avoid over-watering, the drops can be administered daily in a dessertspoonful of water at the usual rate of 4 drops of Rescue and 2 of any other Flower. A tried and tested pick-me-up for cut flowers is a combination of Walnut, Wild Rose and Rescue Remedy. Add 4 drops of Rescue and 2 drops of the other Remedies to an average size vase.

EXTERNAL APPLICATIONS

COMPRESSES

Bach prescribed compresses in addition to internal doses of the Remedies when there were external lesions such as skin eruptions and inflammation. Six drops of Stock are added to half a litre of cold water. Place a small towel, or piece of lint or soft fabric, on the surface of the bowl of water. Wring out the excess and place the compress over the area to be treated. Leave in place until it warms to body heat. Renew as required.

RIGHT REMEDIES CAN ALSO BE USED TO
TREAT PHYSICAL AILMENTS. APPLY A
COMPRESS TO THE SKIN FOR RELIEF
FROM INFLAMMATION.

BATHS

Many Bach Flower users put the Remedies in the bath to augment oral doses of the same Flowers. For example, Olive or Hornbeam for exhaustion, Crab Apple for self-disgust or for skin problems.

FACE WASH OR LOTION

ABOVE AS WELL AS TAKING A REMEDY ORALLY, YOU MAY ALSO WISH TO ADD A FEW DROPS TO YOUR BATHWATER.

For skin complaints such as eczema or teenage spots, Crab Apple is commonly applied externally (combined with other treatment). Fill a 50ml bottle with distilled water or a 50/50 mixture of witch-hazel and distilled water, and add 2 drops of Crab Apple. Shake well before use and apply two or three times daily.

ABOVE DILUTED REMEDIES MAY BE APPLIED TO THE SKIN TO TREAT ECZEMA OR BLEMISHED SKIN.

89

DURATION OF TREATMENT

For acute conditions such as the effects of bad news (Rescue or Star of Bethlehem), that 'Monday morning' feeling (Hornbeam) or fearfulness before an interview (Rescue or Mimulus), take the drops as often as needed. This could be every 15 minutes or so until you feel better. Most people experience some relief almost immediately.

When dealing with deeply ingrained negativity – a domineering and inflexible personality, for example, or a tendency to possessiveness and self-pity – the process of change and a return to health may take many months. As each layer within the psyche begins to peel away, different emotions will emerge, feelings we may have held in check for many years. Make a note of any negative change (of course, positive feelings will also come to the fore) and

USE OF THE RESCUE REMEDY

Rescue Remedy is usually for emergency situations, though it can be used as a long-term Remedy, in place of Star of Bethlehem for instance. For acute conditions such as shock or hysteria, put four drops from the Stock bottle into a cup or glass of water or any other drink. Encourage the person to sip the Remedy at intervals until the distressed feeling abates. The Remedy may also be given neat, directly from the Stock bottle. Put four drops on the tongue as often as required. If the patient is unconscious, the drops can be applied externally, either diluted or directly from the Stock bottle, you should moisten the lips, gums, temples, back of the neck, behind the ears or the wrists.

As a first-aid measure – for example, for sprains, insect stings, bumps and bruises – apply the Remedy neat or diluted in a little water. Alternatively, apply Rescue Remedy Cream.

RIGHT PLACE A FEW DROPS OF RESCUE REMEDY IN A GLASS OF WATER AND SIP REGULARLY UNTIL THE EMOTIONS ARE MORE SETTLED.

BURNS

Burns and scalds should always be cooled immediately under cold running water before applying the liquid Rescue Remedy. Do not use the cream in this instance. The Rescue Remedy given internally will, of course, deal with the shock. Serious burns need urgent medical attention.

LEFT ALWAYS COOL A BURN WITH COLD WATER BEFORE APPLYING RESCUE REMEDY.

add the appropriate Remedy to the treatment bottle. There is no need to prepare a new bottle every time as a 30ml treatment bottle will last for about three weeks, but after a while it may be necessary to reassess the condition and to prescribe accordingly.

An indication of improvement is, of course, when we begin to feel better both physically and mentally and when our family and friends notice the difference – but more especially when we forget to take the Remedies! This means we are becoming less self-interested and beginning to flow outwards to others and the world about us.

EXPERIENCES IN BACH THERAPY

CHAPTER SIX

Bach intended the Flower Remedies to supercede homeopathy proper, and perhaps also to replace some other forms of treatment. He believed that true healing occurred as a result of flooding our being with the light of a higher vibration in the presence of which, disease – as well as the spiritual need for its existence – is eliminated. The Flower Remedies in Bach's own hands undoubtedly proved most efficacious – indeed, almost miraculous on occasions. However, we need to consider how much of this can be attributed to Bach's own extraordinary gift of healing, and how much to the Flower Remedies themselves. In my own experience, which is mirrored by the experiences of many other therapists of different schools of healing, the Flower Remedies cannot totally negate the need for homeopathy, or any other form of treatment for that matter, especially in serious or chronic illness. Nevertheless, the Remedies are extremely supportive, and on occasions can be sufficient in themselves, as the following brief case studies illustrate.

ABOVE ALTHOUGH DR BACH BELIEVED FLOWER REMEDIES WOULD NEGATE THE NEED FOR HOMEOPATHY, THE TWO THERAPIES ARE OFTEN USED TOGETHER.

CASE STUDY 1

Michael is in his mid-30s. At the time of the consultation he was suffering from excruciating lower back pain as a result of hard physical labour. He also mentioned that he had strained his back in a similar manner on several other occasions. Although he believed his problem to be entirely physical in origin, he had been feeling tense and anxious for some days before the accident. Yet again, he had received notice of redundancy from his work in conservation (the third time in two years).

Treatment began with aromatherapy massage. Michael was extremely tense; the muscles of his lower back were in spasm, and his neck and shoulders were tight and painful. He expressed the need to get better quickly as he disliked taking sick leave. I felt that he was not responding to my touch, and so at this point I interrupted the massage (not usually a good practice as it breaks the all-important flow) to give him a glass of water containing Impatiens for his irritability, tension and impatience to return to work; Chestnut Bud, because he had not learnt from past experiences of over-exertion; and Star of Bethlehem for the shock of losing his job.

Almost immediately I detected a change. He began to relax into the massage instead of fighting against it, his breathing deepened and he became very sleepy. At the end of the treatment the pain had eased considerably. Within two weeks of taking the Flower Remedies three or four times a day,

ABOVE IF A PATIENT IS MENTALLY RESISTING MASSAGE, TRY GIVING THEM A DOSE OF A SUITABLE FLOWER REMEDY.

and receiving aromatherapy treatments twice weekly, he began to feel more optimistic. Careerwise, he has decided to go it alone – to run courses and workshops on conservation. Whenever doubt sets in he takes a dose of Gentian to keep him on the right track.

CASE STUDY 2

When I first met Judy she was struggling against all odds to hold down her job as a laboratory technician. At the age of 32, she had been on Valium and anti-depressant drugs for nearly six years, from the time that she had suffered a breakdown and subsequent hospitalization. Her story revealed an unhappy childhood, numerous love affairs in which she was usually the rejected partner and a period during which she experimented with various kinds of intoxicant. She expressed a need to be in more control of her own life, for she felt like a piece of driftwood on a turbulent sea.

Judy's journey towards peace of mind was long and not without pain and setback. However, within nine months she was beginning to see the light at the end of the tunnel.

She had been receiving aromatherapy massage once or twice a month, as well as counselling, relaxation therapy and the Bach Flower Remedies. With her doctor's permission, and with the support of the self-help group Narcotics Anonymous, she managed to give up Valium and to reduce the dosage of the anti-

ABOVE TREATMENT WITH VARIOUS BACH REMEDIES DIMINISHED JUDY'S RELIANCE ON PRESCRIPTION DRUGS.

depressant drug she was taking, though she experienced some harrowing withdrawal symptoms from the Valium.

A number of Remedies were given at various stages. These included Star of Bethlehem for past trauma and shock; Larch for lack of confidence; Mimulus for her fears; Cherry Plum and Gentian when she suffered a serious set-back and feared another breakdown. Scleranthus helped with the mood swings and unsteady gait experienced as a result of withdrawal from Valium; and Agrimony proved useful at times when she found herself putting on an overly cheerful front in order to disguise her inner turmoil from others. However, the most interesting Remedy, the greatest catalyst for change, was revealed through Dreamwork.

Judy had been experiencing a number of dreams centred on the theme of advice-seeking. In one significant dream she found herself consulting an authoritative-looking man dressed in a pin-striped suit. He was seated on a throne. She asked him whether she should sell her car in order to buy a horse. She then found herself mimicking his gestures, facial expression and even the sound of his voice, but when she awoke she could not remember the answer to her question.

The Remedy that sprang to mind was Cerato, the Remedy for the compulsive seeker of advice who ignores the wisdom of his own inner voice, and who also tends to mimic those whom he admires.

A few months later Judy had re-discovered her 'green fingers', and gave up her job to become a self-employed gardener. She was also offered psychotherapy on the NHS, which she was pleased to accept.

CASE STUDY 3

Sylvester, my unneutered tom-cat, was diagnosed with feline AIDS by the vet, though this was not confirmed by a blood test. At any rate, he was seriously ill and not expected to survive another week. However, I was not prepared to say goodbye to my friend, and I felt that he too was not quite ready to take his leave. Healing was geared to nurturing both the physical and the spiritual aspects. The Flower Remedies played an important role, especially Olive and Rescue Remedy, along with homeopathic doses of Sulphur and Arsenicum album at different stages of the illness. Admittedly, this was a hit-or-miss affair as I am not a homeopath. Essential oil of Tea Tree (an anti-viral oil used in the holistic treatment of human AIDS sufferers), was rubbed into his belly every other day. He was also given spiritual healing.

Within a week he began to show signs of recovery. Six months later, Sylvester was his lively mischievous self again.

ABOVE SYLVESTER RESPONDED WELL TO A VARIETY OF HOLISTIC TREATMENTS, INCLUDING RESCUE REMEDY.

TOWARDS WHOLE HEALTH

CHAPTER SEVEN

According to the principles of nature cure (naturopathy) – and indeed of holistic therapy in general – the food we eat, the water we drink, the air we breathe, the seasons and even the phases of the Moon can affect the way we feel. Therefore, by influencing our moods, these things must also affect our physical state.

In truth, as Bach said, 'Nothing can hurt us when we are happy and in harmony.' However, perfect equilibrium between mind, body and spirit is not easy to attain – at least not as a permanent state of being. Yogis and great spiritual teachers have achieved such an ideal, but most of us will be held in check by many factors such as lack of incentive, weakness, heredity, karma (fate or destiny) or whatever.

RIGHT A WELL-BALANCED AND NOURISHING WHOLEFOOD DIET CAN HAVE A POSITIVE EFFECT ON BOTH OUR BODY AND OUR MIND.

The key to good health and a sense of well-being lies in the realization that we need not be helpless victims of stress or distress, which account for a great many ills. While our diet and lifestyle play a part, we need also to nurture our spiritual aspect, for we are more than a mind and a body.

The spiritual aspect is hard to define but is tied up with our relationship with ourselves, with other people, with our own sense of purpose and meaning, and indeed with the health of our Planet. Without purpose we become depressed or apathetic; life then appears bleak and meaningless.

The vision of the truly holistic healer (which must include Bach), is that the expression of such qualities as compassion, intuition and nurturing will raise the consciousness of humanity as a whole. In so doing, we will once again begin to honour the Earth, as did the healers of antiquity, realizing that we and the Earth move together in the one Dance of Life.

The rest of this chapter is devoted to outlining some suggestions for creating favourable conditions within every level of our being, for in so doing we may enhance the action of the Flower Remedies.

THE NATURE OF STRESS

Humans need a high level of stimulation to motivate us and keep us going. Indeed, without 'the spice of life' we begin to feel despondent or apathetic – remember Wild Rose? Conversely, when the demands of life exceed our ability to cope effectively, we begin to suffer the effects of overload. In either situation, we experience distress, which can pave the way towards illness.

Stress is not so much the outside pressures and problems that impinge upon us but rather how we react to those things or people 'out there'. We all know people who remain cool, calm, and collected under the most trying circumstances, and we know others who collapse under the strain of even relatively minor difficulties. The

RIGHT REGULAR EXERCISE IS AN IDEAL WAY TO COMBAT THE STRESSES OF MODERN-DAY LIFE.

trick is to find and maintain just the right level of stress to make our life interesting and fulfilling, and, of course, this balance will be different for each individual.

If your life is understimulating, make every effort to break the routine. Visit new places; follow up sudden notions; take up a new hobby; walk, cycle, swim and so forth.

Exercise has a definite positive effect on our state of mind. Anyone who has recently taken up some form of exercise, especially something they actively enjoy, will tell you that it has brought them enhanced mental energy and con-centration, the ability to sleep more deeply and a feeling of well-being.

If you are elderly, physically disabled or too ill to take exercise, regular mass-age can be of enormous benefit to body, mind and spirit.

99

NATURE ATTUNEMENT

Nature in her myriad forms is perhaps the most potent de-stresser of all – a simple fact so often over-looked by many experts in the field of 'stress management'. She offers tranquillity to the frenzied, and raises the spirits of the down-hearted. All that she asks in return is a little of our time and attention.

Although we may love city life with all its distractions, we can, without realizing it, become very much out of balance when cut off from the natural Earth currents. If you can only occasionally leave the city in order to visit the countryside, sea or mountains, do not despair – even the local park can be a source of healing. Try to take time out each day to breathe in the scents of flowers, trees and grasses, to listen to the birds, to feel the rough bark of a gnarled oak, to walk on the soft earth and to embrace the elements.

In traditional Native American society, if someone became ill, one of the first things they did was to enter the forest where they would sit with their back against the trunk of a mature tree. In this way they 'grounded' themselves, believing that they were 'sitting in the lap of Mother' as they put it, to receive healing. Likewise, we too can benefit from this simple practice.

Incidentally, if you are taking one of the tree Remedies (Oak, Hornbeam, Red Chestnut, etc.) try to find the appropriate tree with which to attune. Breathe deeply and allow yourself to merge with the energies of the tree. Similarly, you can attune to the vibrations of any other Remedy plant such as Gorse, Mimulus, Impatiens or Honeysuckle. Even when not in bloom, silent contemplation of the plant or tree can be a healing experience.

Silent contemplation of moving water is another beautiful attunement. Close your eyes and listen to the music of a running stream, flowing river, waterfall or the waves of the sea. If you live far from any natural source of running water, an ornamental fountain in a park or garden can be of equal value.

For the physically able, what better way is there to commune with nature than to spend some time in the wilderness? There is something special about climbing a mountain, especially for the first time, or camping on the edge of a forest by a running stream, or walking on the remote high cliffs in summertime – feeling the wind in your hair, smelling the scent of wild flowers, experiencing the springy turf underfoot and the air resonating with the symphony of seabirds and crashing waves.

SEEKING WITHIN

As well as communing with nature, you may also enjoy practising a more conscious form of mind/body healing in the form of deep breathing, relaxation, visualization and meditation.

By learning to connect with your inner powers you will tap a source of self-healing that will resonate in harmony with the Bach Flower vibrations. After a while, you will begin to find that you are reacting less self-destructively to the pressures of life, becoming more resourceful in the face of adversity. It is a fact that the mind/body can either trap or liberate the spiritual aspect of self. The condition of spiritual imprisonment or freedom depends on many interrelated factors, but especially on how we breathe and think. Although we may not always be able to change our outer situation, we can change our attitude to it, which makes all the difference in the world:

ABOVE VISUALIZATION MAY ACT AS A POTENT DE-STRESSER, HELPING YOU TO GET IN CONTACT WITH YOUR INNER POWERS OF SELF-HEALING.

> *'Two men look out through prison bars,*
> *the one sees mud, the other stars...'*
> ANON

BREATHING

The power of the breath has always been associated with an energy of both a physical and a metaphysical kind. According to the yogis, the breath is the key to spiritual transformation. Even in the Bible, the word translated as 'spirit' can also be translated as 'air'. It is the invisible life-force. To the Chinese, who attempt to manipulate it in acupuncture, it is *chi*; to the Aborigine, it is *kuranita*; to the Polynesian, it is *manas*; to the yogi, it is *prana*.

By influencing our breathing, we can change our energy levels and our mood. To illustrate this, start to breathe shallowly; pant in and out very quickly for about half-a-minute. At the end of this time you will feel decidedly anxious – your heart will be pounding and you may even be experiencing fear. As an antidote, take three or four long, deep breaths from the abdomen and exhale slowly. You will find your mind and body sinking into a state of calm.

Many of us are shallow breathers; we use only the upper part of our lungs, which means that toxic residues are not completely removed. As a result, our blood is deprived of much of the oxygen it needs to feed the body tissues, so we may end up feeling listless or suffering vagueness of thought. At the same time, the oxygen deficit hinders the assimilation of nutrients from the food we eat.

One of the easiest ways to begin learning to breathe fully, is to practise the yoga 'complete breath'. This exercise is also very beneficial to those suffering from respiratory ailments such as asthma, hay fever and bronchitis.

1   Lie on a rug on the floor or alternatively on a firm bed, or on the ground if outside, with your arms at your sides, several centimetres away from your body, palms facing down.

2   Close your eyes and begin to inhale very slowly through your nose. Expand your abdomen slightly, then pull the air up into the rib-cage, and then your chest. Your abdomen will be drawn in as the ribs move out and the chest expands. Hold for a few seconds.

3   Now begin to breathe out slowly through your nose in a smooth continuous flow until the abdomen is drawn in and the rib-cage and chest are relaxed. Hold for a few seconds before repeating two or three times.

4   Now breathe in slowly as in Step 1 but gradually raise your arms overhead in time with the inhalation until the backs of your hands touch the floor.

5   Hold your breath for ten seconds while you have a good stretch, from fingertips to toes.

6   Slowly breathe out as you bring your arms back down to your sides. Repeat two or three times.

This exercise can also be performed whilst standing. To enhance the stretch (Step 5) stand on tiptoes, your heels coming back down again as you breathe out.

DEEP RELAXATION

Deep relaxation is a prerequisite to the art of visualization and meditation. By inducing a slight shift in consciousness, deep relaxation enhances our ability to concentrate and to use imagery for self-healing – and indeed for the healing of others.

Before you begin, find a quiet, well-ventilated room with a pleasantly relaxing decor. Wear loose, comfortable clothing and take off your shoes. If you live in a noisy area, it may also be helpful to play gentle music, but keep the volume down very low as your senses will be especially acute. Make sure that you will not be disturbed for at least 15 minutes.

1   Lie down on the floor or on a firm bed, supported by pillows if desired – one under your head and another under your knees to support your lower back.

2   Close your eyes, take one or two deep breaths through the nose, then breathe out through the mouth with a sigh.

3   Now become aware of your feet. Inhale deeply through the nose, tighten your feet by first pointing your toes, and then flexing the feet towards your body. Hold on to this tension for a slow count of five, then let your feet relax as you breathe out through the mouth with a deep sigh.

4   As you inhale, tense your calves as you count slowly to five. Now let them relax as you breathe out with a sigh.

5   Progress to your knees, then your thighs, buttocks, abdomen,

chest, shoulders, hands, arms, neck, head and face. Tense each part as you hold the breath, then let it go as you breathe out with a sigh through the mouth, experiencing a wonderful sensation of release.

6 Take three deep breaths, inhaling from the abdomen, but without straining. Hold each breath for a few seconds, then slowly exhale through the nose.

7 Now become aware of your body and 'feel' around your body with your mind for any areas that may still be tense. Repeat the tightening and releasing of the muscles until you feel deeply relaxed and at peace.

8 When you feel ready (after at least five minutes of lying quietly and breathing normally), have a good stretch from fingertips to toes before slowly getting up.

This deep relaxation exercise is most beneficial if practised once or twice a day on an empty stomach, or at least half-an-hour after eating a light meal or snack.

PSYCHIC PROTECTION

Even though we may choose to overlook the fact, to a greater or lesser degree, we humans are sensitive to the energy fields of others in our sphere. How often for instance, have you felt inexplicably uneasy in the presence of another person? Conversely, have you ever experienced a sense of joy, or been uplifted in the company of an unusually vibrant person?

The energy field that surrounds us acts as a filter, allowing only that which cannot harm us to enter. By learning to strengthen our own vibrations, we help to uplift the spirits of those who may seek our help.

We will still be sensitive to atmospheres and to the needs of others, but we will not absorb negativity like a psychic sponge, thus draining our own energies in the process.

STRENGTHENING THE AURA

The aura is largely a thought emanation and as such can easily be controlled by thought. It is often helpful to begin learning to control and strengthen the aura immediately after practising the complete breath and/or the relaxation sequence outlined earlier.

Whilst standing, or lying on your back, close your eyes and take a few long, slow, deep breaths. Then imagine that you are centred within a sphere of white light that also permeates your body. Feel that you are protected within this sphere of light like the yolk within an egg and that the energy around you is unbroken, especially over your head. Some people think of blue or golden light; others may not think of a colour at all but just feel they are centred within a sphere.

With practice, this visualization, or feeling, of your auric space will become second nature. It can be carried out at any time you feel the need without first having to do the breathing or relaxation exercises. Think of your aura when you are near anyone with a cold or flu; when you or others are indulging in negative emotions; in noisy surroundings; first thing in the morning and last thing at night; after meditating or giving Bach Flower counselling.

Another way to dissipate uncomfortable feelings absorbed from others is to take a dose of Rescue Remedy and Walnut in a glass of water. In fact, water itself helps to cleanse the aura, so a bath or shower will also be helpful. Alternatively, dig the garden or go for a brisk walk in the park or countryside – the Earth will absorb or 'ground' any lingering discomfort.

CREATING A HEALING CHANNEL

If it feels appropriate to you, the following visualization will be most helpful if practised a few minutes before each consultation.

1   Either standing or lying down on a firm but comfortable surface, take several complete breaths (*see* pp.101–102).
2   Close your eyes and think of your aura as in the previous exercise. Then imagine that you are centred along a straight line running

from the top of your head to your feet (this is known as 'centring'). Feel perfectly balanced and calm.

3   The next stage is to become a channel of healing energy – not the source as this would only serve to drain your own vitality. To become a channel, imagine (or feel) a source of energy above your head, a ball of white light or the Sun. At this point you can either address your higher self or say a prayer asking that you may draw down cosmic energy (or be given the ability) to help the person in the way best suited to their specific needs.

4   Now take a few deep breaths. As you inhale, imagine you are drawing energy from the source of light, in through the top of your head, and out through your hands and feet as you exhale.

During the consultation, you might also find it helpful to imagine that you are both centred within the same sphere of white light (some therapists prefer to imagine a triangle) above which is placed a symbol of protection. Symbols most commonly used include an equidistant cross within a circle, a white rose, or an ankh (a symbol of eternal life). The visualization can be carried out in an instant, without its being obvious to the other person (not everyone will feel comfortable with this approach). However, if the person is amenable to intuitive healing, all well and good. They too can think of their own aura, and then merge their energies within the greater sphere or triangle of light.

At the end of the consultation, send a closing thought to the other person; see that they are separate from yourself, safely enclosed within their own spiritual sphere.

Now separate and ground yourself; that is, think of your own aura, see yourself centred along a straight line as before, then become aware of your feet in contact with the ground. If necessary, excuse yourself for a few moments in order to carry out this visualization.

The power of thought is everything. If you are able to do this successfully, and if there is an empathy between yourself and the other person, not only will your intuition and counselling skills be enhanced, but the experience will be healing for both parties.

REFLECTIVE MEDITATION

This is an active form of meditation as taught by the Pegasus Foundation (my own teachers) based in Malvern, England. Many Eastern approaches are passive in that they aim either to empty the mind or help us to become observers of our own thoughts – a difficult task for the beginner. Reflective meditation, on the other hand, involves thinking about a definite subject, theme, thought or word.

The following meditation can be recorded on to tape, but do allow plenty of pauses for the visualizations marked thus: ... Or you might be able to persuade a friend with a soothing voice to guide you through it. Meditation should ideally be practised for 15–20 minutes daily, preferably first thing in the morning. However, even as little as two or three sessions a week can help to reduce stress, improve concentration and encourage creativity and inspiration.

Before you begin, sit comfortably in a quiet room or in a garden. A cross-legged position may be adopted if you are accustomed to this position, otherwise sit in a straight-backed chair with your feet firmly on the ground and your hands resting in your lap.

1   Close your eyes. Empty your lungs and begin to breathe deeply through your nose. Do not strain, just try to become aware of the breath as it flows in and out. Do this for two minutes.

ABOVE REGULAR MEDITATION PRACTICE CAN BRING HAPPINESS, HARMONY AND INNER PEACE.

2   Concentrate on your feet; let them go, thinking relaxation into them... now move over every part of your body in turn, letting go and relaxing your calves... knees... thighs... hips... abdomen... now your chest... hands and arms... shoulders... neck... now your face... your eyes... your forehead... your scalp... even your tongue.

3   Now feel that you are centred within a sphere of white light – your aura.

4   Picture a majestic gnarled Oak standing in a lush green meadow; tall, strong and in full leaf. See the width of its deeply furrowed trunk; the dark hollow in its base – the hiding place of many a small child. Look up into the dark green canopy. Consider how this ancient giant grew from a tiny acorn over many years; how its ancestors provided fruit for the wild boar, fuel and shelter for human beings. There is yet another gift from the Oak – a most precious gift that emanates from its pale yellow catkin flowers – a power to heal and comfort you when the responsibilities of life become a burden too great to bear alone. The Oak bestows upon you the virtue of strength in the face of adversity, helping you to overcome all life's uncertainties with courage and steadfastness.

5   Now feel the rough bark of the Oak... In that roughness there is a soft smile, a gentle smile like that of a loving, weatherbeaten father who has worked hard to protect you, child of the Oak...

6   Move closer and closer to the trunk of the tree until you finally become absorbed into it... You are no longer observing the Oak for you are now it. You stand tall and strong. You feel movement in your branches. Listen now to the symphony of birds, insects and red squirrels as they play, safe within your fatherly embrace... Breathe deeply, purify the air through your leaves... Radiate emerald green light so that every living being of the Earth may be healed... Become aware of your roots; feel how they reach down into the dark moist soil, spreading far like your branches, anchoring you to the Earth. Experience stillness... Only your leaves are stirred by the dance of the warm breeze and the soft summer rain.

7   Now it is time gradually to separate your consciousness from that of the tree. Step aside. See that the Oak stands before you. Feel its shelter for a moment before allowing the picture to recede into the distance... You are yourself once again.

8   Direct your consciousness back into your body. Imagine yourself centred along a straight line running from the top of your head to your feet. . . Feel safely enclosed within your sphere of light.

9   Open your eyes. Shake out your limbs and have a good stretch from fingertips to toes.

You might also like to meditate on any of the other Flower Remedy plants or trees. Follow the same format as with the Oak meditation. Carry out Steps 1–3, then direct your attention to the subject. See the plant or tree clearly in your mind; observe it, consider its healing virtues. Reach out to touch the bark of the tree, or the cool silky petals of the flower; smell the scent of Pine or of Honeysuckle. Identify yourself with the plant or tree – you are no longer thinking about it because you are it. Finally, gradually withdraw from the form of your subject; see it once more as separate from yourself, and then direct your consciousness back into your body as in Steps 7–9.

AND FINALLY...

'We are all healers, and with love and sympathy in our natures we are also able to help anyone who really desires health. Seek for the outstanding mental conflict in the patient, give him the remedy that will assist him to overcome that particular fault, and all the encouragement and hope you can, and then the healing virtue within him will of itself do the rest.'

DR EDWARD BACH

AT-A-GLANCE REFERENCE CHARTS

SUMMARY OF USES OF FLOWER REMEDIES

Where there is doubt, the following reference should help. However, this chart is meant only as a prompt and should always be used in conjunction with the fuller descriptions presented in chapter 4. With each flower remedy, the mood and personality type is given.

AGRIMONY: cheerfulness conceals inner torment; fears being alone; anxious; avoids arguments; rarely complains; weak-willed on occasions; desires excitement; fears illness; restless; sapped by others; suicidal tendencies.

ASPEN: fear of some impending evil; delusions; night terrors; suicidal tendencies; ungrounded; sometimes psychic.

AGRIMONY

BEECH: criticizes others; arrogant; has high ideals; irritable; rigid in mind and body; incapable of sympathy for others; strong willed.

CENTAURY: subservient; a willing drudge; self-denial; conventional; sapped by others; over-sensitive; sometimes mediumistic.

CERATO: always seeking advice; greedy for information; changeable; fussy; saps others; imitative; lacks concentration; conventional; easily dominated; foolish.

CHERRY PLUM: fears insanity; subject to delusions; feels desperate; has suicidal tendencies; fears harming self or others; nervous breakdown; violent temperament through fear.

CHESTNUT BUD: fails to learn from past mistakes; lacks observation; a slow learner; thoughts often in the future.

CHICORY: possessive (of people and things); dislikes being alone; enjoys arguments; domineering; fussy; mentally congested; fears losing friends; fretful; feigns illness to obtain sympathy; may use emotional blackmail; anxious; self-centred; tearful; strong willed; saps others; house proud.

111

CLEMATIS: absent-minded; daydreams; lacks ambition; apathetic; welcomes prospect of death; ungrounded; lacks vitality; impractical; needs much sleep; imaginative; thoughts in the future; feigns illness to escape from life; sapped by others; uncomplaining; often artistic; sometimes mediumistic.

CRAB APPLE: self-disgust; over-attention to detail; feels unclean; fussy; house proud; anxious; may have a skin complaint.

ELM: despondent through feelings of inadequacy; feels discouraged though usually copes well.

GENTIAN: depressed through set-back; 'doubting Thomas' attitude.

GORSE: feels depressed through feelings of hopelessness; can be persuaded to try again, albeit halfheartedly; may be chronically ill.

HEATHER: self-centred; talkative; saps others; feigns illness to obtain sympathy; dislikes being alone; often lonely; mentally congested; over anxious for self; childish; weeps easily.

HOLLY: jealous; full of hate; resentful; angry; finds fault with others; violent temperament; suspicious; saps others.

HONEYSUCKLE

HONEYSUCKLE: nostalgic; lives in the past; absent-minded; day dreams; drowsy; homesick; lacks observation; often talkative; sad; saps others.

HORNBEAM: uncertain through lack of strength; tired; bored; lazy (that 'Monday morning' feeling).

112

IMPATIENS: impatient; irritable; desires to work alone at own swift pace; over-works; has high ideals; self-sufficient; finds fault with others; quick in mind and body; suffers nervous tension; sometimes angry or violent.

LARCH: lacks confidence; expects failure; hesitant; feigns illness to avoid responsibility; weak-willed; may also suffer from impotence.

MIMULUS: nervous by nature; fears known things such as loneliness, poverty, visiting the dentist, animals, parties, speaking in public, etc; shy; lacks confidence; over sensitive to noise, strife and controversy; has suicidal tendencies; sometimes talkative; sapped by others; easily dominated.

MIMULUS

MUSTARD: feels depression like a black cloud, the cause unknown, often cyclic in nature.

OAK: carries a burden in life; a plodder against all odds; annoyed on account of illness; discontented with self; rarely complains; may suffer nervous breakdown or collapse; violent temperament through instability.

OLIVE: lacks effort due to physical and emotional exhaustion; fears losing friends; no pleasure in life.

OAK

PINE: feels guilt, despair, self-reproach; blames self for the wrong doings of others.

RED CHESTNUT: over-concern for others; absence of fear for self; always imagines the worst; distressed by reports of war, famine or other disasters; mentally congested; tense.

ROCK ROSE: (also Rescue Remedy) feels extreme fear, terror or panic – enough to cause fear in those around; nightmares; life or death situations.

ROCK WATER: hard master to self; self-denial; likes to be a good example to others; self-critical; has fixed ideas and opinions; a perfectionist; intolerant, but rarely openly critical of others; self-martyrdom; anxious; tense; strong-willed.

SCLERANTHUS: alternating moods; indecisive; unreliable; lacks concentration; lacks confidence; weak convictions; hesitant; unstable; may suffer nervous breakdown or collapse; lacks poise; restless; may have a violent temperament.

STAR OF BETHLEHEM: (also Rescue Remedy) emotional and physical shock; deep-rooted problems due to past trauma; grief; emotional numbness; refuses to be consoled; tense.

SWEET CHESTNUT: extreme anguish, so great as to seem unbearable; utter despair; unable even to pray.

VERVAIN: over-enthusiastic; missionary zeal; enjoys argument and debate; strong-willed; interferes in the affairs of others; over-effort; rigid in mind and body; impulsive; intolerant; a martyr to the cause; may suffer nervous breakdown or collapse; nervy; quick in mind and body; talkative.

VINE: dictatorial; ruthlessly ambitious; strong-willed; hard master to others; intolerant; lacks sympathy for others; violent temperament; born to lead.

VINE

114

WALNUT: difficulty in severing old ties; has definite ambition, finds transition difficult, sometimes held back or misguided by others; feels frustration.

WATER VIOLET: proud and aloof; suffers in silence; physical rigidity; self-reliant; desires to be alone; avoids argument; poised; sad; radiates superiority.

WHITE CHESTNUT:
tormented by mental arguments; carousel mind; may suffer from insomnia; lacks observation; worried.

WILD OAT: dissatisfaction through unfulfilled ambition; uncertain about the future; sometimes a 'Jack of all trades, master of none'; unable to settle down.

WILD ROSE: apathetic (the cause often unknown); weary; gloomy; uncomplaining; dislikes change; 'I'll have to live with it' attitude.

WILLOW: 'poor me' attitude; bitter and resentful; selfish; enjoys arguments; blames others; grumpy; morose; may simulate illness to obtain pity; irritable; sulky.

FINDING A FLOWER REMEDY FOR YOUR MENTAL STATE

As with the previous chart, the following reference will serve as a useful prompt, but should always be used in conjunction with the flower essence profiles in Chapter 4. With each flower remedy, the mood and personality type is given.

ABSENT-MINDEDNESS: Chestnut Bud, Clematis, Honeysuckle, Mustard, Olive, White Chestnut, Wild Rose

ADDICTION: (TO SUBSTANCES/LIMITATION/INDIVIDUALS): Agrimony, Aspen, Chestnut Bud, Clematis

AGGRESSION: Cherry Plum, Holly, Impatiens, Rescue Remedy, Scleranthus, Vine

ALOOFNESS: Rock Water, Water Violet

AMBIVALENCE: Cerato, Scleranthus, Wild Oat

ANGER: Cherry Plum, Holly, Impatiens, Rescue Remedy, Vine

CERATO

ANXIETY: Agrimony, Aspen, Cerato, Chicory, Cherry Plum, Crab Apple, Elm, Heather, Larch, Mimulus, Red Chestnut, Rescue Remedy, Rock Water, White Chestnut

APATHY: Clematis, Gorse, Wild Rose

ARGUMENTATIVENESS: Beech, Chicory, Holly, Impatiens, Vervain, Vine, Willow

ARROGANCE: Beech, Vine

BEMUSED, FEELING OF BEING: Clematis, Rescue Remedy

BOREDOM: Hornbeam

BROKEN-HEARTEDNESS: Clematis, Holly, Honeysuckle, Rescue Remedy, Star of Bethlehem, Sweet Chestnut, Wild Rose, Willow

CONFIDENCE, LACK OF: Cerato, Centaury, Elm, Larch, Pine

DELUSIONS: Aspen, Cherry Plum, Rescue Remedy

GORSE

DEPRESSION: Gentian, Gorse, Mustard, Sweet Chestnut, Wild Rose

DESPONDENCY AND DESPAIR: Crab Apple, Elm, Larch, Oak, Pine, Star of Bethlehem, Sweet Chestnut, Willow

DEVITALIZATION: Olive

DISDAINFULNESS: Beech, Crab Apple, Rock Water, Water Violet

DISORIENTATION: Clematis, Honeysuckle, Rescue Remedy, Scleranthus

DOMINEERING, DESIRE TO BE: Chicory, Vervain, Vine

EGOTISM: Beech, Chicory, Holly, Water Violet

EASILY LED, BEING: Agrimony, Centaury, Cerato, Chestnut Bud, Walnut

117

EMOTIONAL BLACKMAIL (TO OBTAIN PITY): Chicory, Willow

ESCAPISM: Agrimony, Clematis, Chestnut Bud, Honeysuckle, Water Violet, Wild Oat

CHESTNUT

FANATICISM: Vervain, Vine

FEAR: Aspen, Cherry Plum, Mimulus, Red Chestnut, Rescue Remedy, Rock Rose

FRUSTRATION: Gentian, Impatiens

FUSSINESS: Cerato, Chicory, Crab Apple, Beech

GRIEF (SEE BROKEN-HEARTEDNESS)

GUILT: Pine

HATRED: Holly, Willow

HOMESICKNESS: Honeysuckle

HOPELESSNESS: Gorse, Sweet Chestnut, Wild Rose

HYSTERIA: Rescue Remedy, Rock Rose

IDEALISM: Elm, Rock Water, Vervain

IMITATIVE, BEING: Cerato

IMPULSIVENESS: Impatiens, Vervain

INDECISIVENESS: Cerato, Larch, Scleranthus, Wild Oat

INERTIA: Chestnut Bud, Hornbeam

SCLERANTHUS

INNER TORMENT: Agrimony

INSECURITY: Aspen, Larch, Mimulus, Wild Oat

INSOMNIA (SEE ALSO WORRY): Rescue Remedy, White Chestnut

INTOLERANCE: Beech, Impatiens, Rock Water, Vervain, Vine, Willow

IRRITABILITY: Beech, Chicory, Crab Apple, Impatiens, Willow

JEALOUSY: Holly

LONELINESS: Beech, Chicory, Elm, Heather, Holly, Honeysuckle, Impatiens, Mustard, Sweet Chestnut, Water Violet

MENTAL CONGESTION: Heather, Rescue Remedy, White Chestnut

MISERLINESS: Chicory, Willow

MONOTONOUS EXISTENCE: Centaury, Gentian, Wild Rose

MOOD-SWINGS: Rescue Remedy, Scleranthus

NERVOUS BREAKDOWN: Cherry Plum, Oak, Rescue Remedy, Vervain

NERVY, BEING: Aspen, Cherry Plum, Impatiens, Mimulus, Rescue Remedy, Vervain

NIGHTMARES: Aspen, Cherry Plum, Rescue Remedy, Rock Rose

HONEYSUCKLE

119

NOSTALGIA: Honeysuckle

OVER-CRITICAL, TENDENCY TO BEING: Beech, Chicory, Vine

OVER-SENSITIVITY: Aspen, Beech, Centaury, Crab Apple, Mimulus, Red Chestnut, Rescue Remedy, Star of Bethlehem, Walnut

OVERWHELMED, FEELING OF BEING: Cherry Plum, Elm, Hornbeam, Oak, Rescue Remedy, Sweet Chestnut

OVERWORK: Elm, Impatiens, Oak, Rescue Remedy

PARANOIA: Aspen, Holly

PERFECTIONISM: Agrimony, Beech, Crab Apple, Elm, Rock Water, Water Violet

PESSIMISM: Gentian, Gorse, Larch

PHOBIAS: Mimulus, Rescue Remedy

POSSESSIVENESS: Chicory, Heather, Red Chestnut

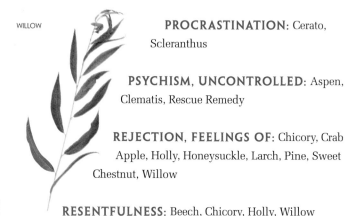

WILLOW

PROCRASTINATION: Cerato, Scleranthus

PSYCHISM, UNCONTROLLED: Aspen, Clematis, Rescue Remedy

REJECTION, FEELINGS OF: Chicory, Crab Apple, Holly, Honeysuckle, Larch, Pine, Sweet Chestnut, Willow

RESENTFULNESS: Beech, Chicory, Holly, Willow

RESTLESSNESS: Agrimony, Impatiens, Vervain, White Chestnut, Wild Oat

SAPPED BY OTHERS, BEING: Agrimony, Centaury, Clematis, Mimulus

SAP OTHERS, TENDENCY TO: Cerato, Chicory, Heather, Holly, Honeysuckle

SELF-AGGRANDIZEMENT: Beech, Vine, Water Violet

SELF-CENTREDNESS: Beech, Chicory, Heather, Vine, Willow

SELF-CRITICISM: Crab Apple, Rock Water

SELF-DECEPTION: Agrimony

SELF-DISGUST: Crab Apple

SELF-EFFACEMENT: Centaury, Pine

SELFISHNESS: Chicory, Heather, Holly

SELF-MARTYRDOM: Centaury,
Rock Water

SELF-PITY: Chicory, Willow

SHAME: Agrimony, Crab Apple, Larch, Pine

SHOCK: Rescue Remedy, Star of Bethlehem

STAR OF BETHLEHEM

STRESS: Cherry Plum, Elm, Impatiens, Olive, Rescue Remedy,
Star of Bethlehem, Vervain

121

SUBSERVIENCE: Centaury

SUICIDAL TENDENCIES: Agrimony, Cherry Plum, Mimulus, Rescue
Remedy

SUPPRESSED EMOTION: Agrimony, Beech, Rock Water, Water Violet

SUSPICIOUSNESS: Holly

TEMPER TANTRUM: Cherry Plum, Holly, Impatiens, Rescue Remedy

TENSION: Impatiens, Rescue Remedy, Rock Water, Vervain, Water Violet

UNCERTAINTY: Cerato, Scleranthus

UNFULFILLED AMBITION: Walnut, Wild Oat

UNCONSCIOUSNESS: Clematis, Rescue Remedy

UNGROUNDEDNESS: Aspen, Cherry Plum, Clematis, Honeysuckle, Mimulus, Rescue Remedy, Rock Rose, Scleranthus, Star of Bethlehem, Walnut

UNSYMPATHETIC, FEELING: Beech, Vine, Willow

VIOLENT ACTIONS, THOUGHTS OR DREAMS: Cherry Plum, Holly, Impatiens, Scleranthus, Rescue Remedy, Vine

WEAK WILL: Agrimony, Centaury, Cerato, Larch, Mimulus

ROCK ROSE

WORRY: Agrimony, Aspen, Crab Apple, Elm, Gentian, Mimulus, Mustard, Oak, Red Chestnut, Rescue Remedy, White Chestnut

FURTHER READING

Bach, E. *Heal Thyself*, C.W. Daniel, 1931.

Barnard, J. and Barnard, M. *The Healing Herbs of Edward Bach*, The Flower Remedy Programme, 1988.

Bricklin, Mark *Practical Encyclopaedia of Natural Healing*, Rodale Press, 1976.

Capra, Dr F. *The Tao of Physics*, Flamingo, 1985.

Chancellor, P.M., *Handbook of the Bach Flower Remedies*, C.W. Daniel, 1971.

Chopra, Dr D. *Quantum Healing*, Bantam Books, 1989.

Howard, J. *The Bach Flower Remedies Step by Step*, C.W. Daniel, 1990.

Howard, J. and Ramsell, J. *The Original Writings of Edward Bach*, C.W. Daniel, 1990.

Kaplan-Williams, Strephon *The Elements of Dreamwork*, Element Books, 1996

Kenton, L. *The Biogenic Diet*, Century Arrow, 1986.

Krystal, P. *Cutting the Ties that Bind*, Element Books, 1987.

Scheffer, M. *Bach Flower Therapy*, Thorsons, 1986.

Vlamis, G. *Flowers to the Rescue*, Thorsons, 1986.

Weeks, N. *The Medical Discoveries of Edward Bach, Physician*, C.W. Daniel, 1989.

Wright, C. *The Wright Diet*, Piatkus, 1986.

USEFUL ADDRESSES

SUPPLIERS OF BOOKS and Flower Remedies (mail order), seminars and professional training courses. Please enclose a stamped addressed envelope with all enquiries.

Official Distributors of the Bach Centre

UK
Dr Edward Bach Centre,
Mount Vernon,
Sotwell
Wallingford
Oxfordshire
OX10 0PZ
UK
Tel:1491 834678/8394891

USA/CANADA
Nelson Bach USA
100 Research Drive
Wilmington
MA 01887
Tel:508 988 3833

AUSTRALIA
Martin & Pleasance
Wholesale Pty Ltd.
PO Box 2054
Richmond
Victoria 3121
Tel:942 77422

HOLLAND
T S Reform
Gelreweg 7
An Harderwijk 3843
Tel:03414 26966

DENMARK
Camette
Lillebaelstuej 47
Esbjerg N 6715
Tel:0045 75 47 0555

GERMANY, AUSTRIA, SWITZERLAND
Dr Bach Bluten Essenzen
Lippmanstrasse 53
Hamburg 22769
Germany
Tel:0404 318780

NEW ZEALAND
Weleda
Havelock North
PO Box 8132
Tel:646 87718780

The following organization has no connection with the Bach Centre in Oxfordshire, but their Flower Remedies are prepared from the same plant species, employing the traditional methods as advocated by Dr Bach.

The Flower Remedy Programme
PO Box 65
Hereford HR2 0UW
UK
Tel:1873 890218

Suppliers of other
flower essences
include:
UK
Findhorn Flower
Essences
Mercury
Findhorn Bay
Forres, Moray
Scotland IV36 0TY
Tel: 1309 690129

Healing Herbs Ltd
The Flower Remedy
Programme
PO Box 65
Hereford HR2 0UW
Tel: 1873 890218

USA/CANADA
Flower Essence
Society
PO Box 459
Nevada City
CA 95959
Tel: 800 736 9222
or 530 265 9163

Pacific Essences
Box 8317
Victoria
BC V8W 3R9
Canada

FRANCE
Deva, Elixirs Floraux
Deva
La Laboratoire Deva
BP3
38880 Autrans
Tel: 33 76 95 35 87

For those in need of spiritual healing, counselling or psychotherapy, contact the following organization. Courses and workshops are also available. Please enclose a stamped addressed envelope with all enquiries.

For spiritual healing only, write to the following: organization; they will supply the name, address and telephone number of an accredited healer in your area. Please enclose a stamped addressed envelope.

The Pegasus Foundation
Runnings Park
Croft Bank
West Malvern
Worcestershire
WR14 4DU
UK
Tel:1684 573868

National Federation of
Spiritual Healers
Old Manor Farm Studio
Church Street
Sunbury-on-Thames
Middlesex TW16 6RG
UK
Tel:1932 783164

INDEX

127

128